W9-ABW-987

Holding Your Ground

By Joe Nobody

Plans within this book utilize a spreadsheet available at:

www.PrepperPress.com/Holding

or

www.HoldingYourGround.com

Published by Prepper Press

Publishing to Help You Prepare

Copyright © 2011 by Kemah Bay Marketing LTD.

No part of this book may be reproduced or utilized in any form or by any means, electronic or mechanical, including photocopying, recording, or by any information storage or retrieval system, without permission in writing from Kemah Bay Marketing LTD. Inquiries should be addressed to: Kemah Bay Marketing LTD, 2301 S. Kemah Drive, Kemah, Texas 77565-3173

Introduction

The purpose of this book is to provide instruction, ideas and concepts for protecting your family in the event of a break down in society or services. This book uses scientific facts, historical examples and good old common sense as the basis for the content.

Most people who start preparing for bad times quickly realize that it is practically impossible to address every scenario. There are too many options, too many expenses and too many unknowns. I have met home owners who have made an extensive investment in solar power systems, only to become frustrated when they read that an Electro Magnetic Pulse (EMP) event would probably disable the entire system.

While it is not productive to dwell on all the possible "What if?" scenarios, it is prudent to consider what simple elementary and intermediate steps each of us can take to be in a position to protect our loved ones.

Preparing for the defense of a location is not expensive. Most of the concepts and ideas in this book can be implemented with little or no expense. While the book will cover some very sophisticated equipment as an option, these items are really the exception and not the rule.

The questions generated by preparation activities are typically answered with more questions and a cycle of analysis paralysis quickly ensues. This book attempts to provide methodology and scientific processes to assist the reader with preparation activities in the area of security, or defense of their location. Unfortunately, security has to overlap with other primary needs, such as shelter, water and food. This book will **not** provide you with plans for the construction of an underground bunker, but will provide instruction on how to defend it.

An argument can be made that no other preparations are complete without security plans being in place. If the scenario involves looting or theft, no matter how much food you have stored, it won't do you any good if someone comes in and takes it all.

Preparing, or being a "prepper" as we sometimes refer to ourselves, is not a socially acceptable activity in many circles. Most people don't want their friends or neighbors knowing their beliefs or activities. Most of us consider ourselves "model" citizens and productive members of a society, so the concept of preparing for the decline of said society is not a natural act. Defensive planning and preparation can be performed in the privacy of your own home and with other individuals with whom you share similar beliefs. There is nothing in this book about deploying barbwire barriers across your front yard, or digging siege trenches around your garden, so you don't have to worry about the neighbors thinking you are crazy or radical. The folks down the street are still going to knock on your door in hopes you will support their high school band fundraiser. I can think of no defense against **that**.

History, both recent and ancient, is rife with examples of society breaking down for short periods of time. The lessons learned from the study of these examples are critical in any preparation activities. There are certain commonalities in human behavior whether you study the Dark Ages or New Orleans after Hurricane Katrina.

The concept of security is not focused on firearms but they have to be part of the discussion. There are hundreds of resources concerning firearms and other defensive equipment and skills. How do you decide on what type of weapon is best and how much to invest if you don't understand their place in a total defensive plan? If you are an accomplished shooter or ex-military, you probably already know more about firearms and their capabilities than is covered in this book. What will be covered in detail are the lessons learned and information available from recent conflicts such as those in Iraq and Afghanistan as well as other sources where violence has become common in a population or region.

The process of planning for security is not focused on shelter – but has to address it. A farm requires a significantly different plan and equipment than a location in an urban area. Defending a mobile home is different from defending an underground location.

The level of Security required depends on water and food sources, so they have to be included as well. If your plans involve a backyard garden as a food source, then you had better be prepared to defend that area as you harvest your corn.

Who should read this book?

HOLDING YOUR GROUND is written for people who prepare for a time when two critical situations become reality:

The Government no longer provides security, either locally or nationally.

There is a disruption in the food supply.

The reason or cause really does not matter. It could be natural disasters, economic collapse, social upheaval, EMP attack, pandemic, or any other doomsday scenario you can think of. If law enforcement is no longer there and people are hungry, ugly things can happen.

We preppers are normally peaceful people who simply want to grow our food, raise our children and perhaps contribute to the re-building of our society should such events occur. Unfortunately, not everyone prepares and that means there may be haves and have not's. Every society has some economic division of its people and for the most part, they co-exist without issue. When it comes to FOOD, the chances of a peaceful existence between those who have and those who don't is low. We live in a free, well-armed society, and that means if trouble does erupt - it will probably be violent.

HOLDING uses several military terms and concepts and these can be intimidating for some people. Fortunately for our society, our military and law enforcement have handled the "dirty work" of protecting us for hundreds of years. Since we are planning for a world where they will no longer provide that security, we need to learn some of their skills. They have established a very specific terminology to teach these skills and it works. While I could not justify reinventing their "educational wheel", a serious attempt is made to communicate in "laymen's" terms wherever practical. All of us may need to think a little more like a soldier or policeman.

If you are "a little past your prime", *HOLDING* can help you "hide in plain sight" and avoid trouble whenever possible. I fall into this category and while I could still put up a good fight, combat is for younger men. *HOLDING* can teach you how to set up your location (bug out or bug in) so that you can have the best chance of surviving even the worst situations.

If you are part of a young family, *HOLDING* will provide you with several ideas to assist you with your plan and the options available to you. A The End Of The World As We Know It (TEOTWAWKI) life with younger children is a completely different situation than an all-adult group. The potential issues regarding those precious young ones are considered throughout.

If you are part of a large, geographically close family or group, HOLDING will provide valuable information on how to utilize your team's size and capabilities.

Regardless of your age, the size of your group, where you are located and what your physical capabilities are – *HOLDING* can teach you certain basics that may make the difference if it all falls apart.

WARNING

Some of the concepts, ideas, maneuvers and devices included in this book are dangerous and could cause injury or death.

You should not attempt any of these activities without proper training, safety measures and safety equipment being applied and/or implemented.

You agree to hold harmless the publisher, author and all associated with HOLDING YOUR GROUND, regardless of circumstance or event.

By proceeding, you are agreeing to accept full responsibility for your own actions, any results of those actions and thus no liability can be assumed or placed with the publisher, author or anyone associated with HOLDING YOUR GROUND.

Contents

1. Decisions

Before you start to implement any plan for location defense or location security, you have several decisions to make. These choices will define the scope, capabilities and parameters of your defensive plan.

Ultimately, all of this is up to you and your family. Most people build additional capabilities over time. This spreads the investment in both energy and funds over a longer period and almost becomes a hobby for some. As with most "hobbies", the more in-depth or comprehensive, the more investment it requires.

Military planners equip the troops for certain timelines involving their mission. Some missions require enough supplies for three days, while others require ten or more without re-supply. You, like those planners, will have to make the decision about what your plan is going to encompass – or what is the "mission."

These same decisions really apply to any type of preparation. Some people prepare for a long term break-down while others simply want a "Hurricane Bag" or "Earthquake Kit" good for 3-5 days.

Security preparations for short term situations are typically not a large effort. Police, National Guard and eventually regular military will quickly regain control and thus provide some level of security for isolated natural disasters. Long term preparations are more complex and difficult. If you believe there is a possibility of a complete breakdown in society, your plan is going to be more complex.

General Huba Wass de Czege, United States Army (ret) is credited for developing a simple formula to determine the "Combat Power" for a unit of almost any size. The good General's widely accepted formula uses a series of rankings, factors and weighted averages to compute a result. That result allows for commanders to improve areas that are lacking and focus resources where they will provide the best return on investment.

In this book, we will use a very similar method to determine how much "defensive power" or what level of capabilities is required for your defense. It uses weighted values based on **your decisions** as to what **your plan** needs to address.

2. How to Use this Book

HOLDING is divided into five primary sections:

1. A Methodology for Preparing – rules and tests to use before you take steps
2. The Terms – basic terms, phrases and definitions you need to know about defense
3. The Initial Assessment – what is the status of your defensive capabilities right now
4. How to improve your plan – things you can do to increase your capabilities
5. The Author's Plan – To be used as an example and perhaps initiate new thinking

In Section 2, you will be asked to research various facts and fill in the results into either the free worksheet, which can be downloaded at **www.PrepperPress.com/Holding** or **www.HoldingYourGround.com**. You can also do the math manually (*all formulas are in Appendix A*).

You then use the results of your research to help you make informed decisions. Systems Engineers refer to this as "Decision Support." If you are thinking of improving your skills with a firearm, then you can see how the results will improve your plan. At a high level, you can model the effect of any investment of time, funds or energy.

As you progress through the book, you will find dozens of ideas to improve your plan. As you implement these, or your own ideas, you modify the worksheet, and can see the value.

When you see this symbol (left) it indicates there is a potential entry or action to be taken with the worksheet.

You will also use the results of this next section throughout the remainder of the book in order to determine what equipment and supplies you will require in order to accomplish your plan.

So grab a piece of paper and a pencil as you proceed through the following sections.

Location Defense Worksheet

Location Factors	
Population Density	0
Proximity	0
Physical Area	0
Visibility	0
High Ground	0
Positions	0
Open Access	0
Limited Access	0
No Access	0
Location Rating	0.00

Group Factors

Number of Defenders

No Firearms Experience	0
Basic Pistol Experience	0
Basic Rifle Experience	0
Advanced Firearms Experience	0
Long Range Marksman	0
Combat Vet	0
Trained Sniper	0

Condition of Group

Restricted Mobility	0
Mobile	0
Physically Fit	0

Athletic	0
Number of Dependents	0

Special Skills

Basic Medical (First Aid)	0
Medical (RN, EMT)	0
Doctor	0
Hunter	0
Engineer	0
Electronics	0
Machinist, Welder, Handyman	0

Mindset

Timid or Unknown	0
Average	0
Aggressive	0
Has your back	0

Group Rating	0.00

Defensive Preparations

Fighting Positions - Interior	0
Fighting Positions - Exterior	0
Over Watch	0
Defensive Rating	0.00

3. The Methodology of Preparing Your Defense

When it comes to complex objectives, such as the defense of a location, I have found that a proper methodology helps me navigate all of the options, parameters and decisions one is faced with.

Before purchases, plans, practice or even serious thought, I believe strongly in establishing a set of rules, tests and steps to accomplish any goal or solve any problem. This is really not complex if you give it a little consideration.

When it comes to any type of preparation activity, here are the rules and tests that I apply to the process:

i. **Do No Harm** – I will not implement any plan that will <u>harm</u>:
   - The value of my property
   - The lifestyle of my family
   - My moral character
   - My code of life and behavior
   - My position as a law abiding citizen and patriot

ii. **Dual Purpose** – As this book will cover, the likelihood of any of this being necessary is low. Any investment in equipment, time, stress or training should serve a dual purpose. This is so that over the long term, frustration, empathy and *buyer's remorse* do not set in.

   Example: Camping gear can be dual purposed for, of all things, CAMPING! This is a recreational activity, something fun and useful. Since we live in Texas; close enough to the coast that we have to bug-out in case of a hurricane, our Bug Out Bag (BOB) is dual purpose.

iii. **People will be the biggest problem.** So in my methodology, people are to be avoided. Our plans, equipment and supplies are all centered on the emphasis of AVOIDING PEOPLE.

iv. **You and your family are people, and thus, still the biggest problem.** So much has been written about the mental state of survival that I will not be a bore here and repeat it all; however, anything we include in our plans should improve the mental state of my group, or at minimum, not degrade it.

v. **When it comes to equipment or skills, look at the military first.** I have found that military grade equipment is designed to be used by conscripts with little training under high stress conditions. It is also designed to last for long periods of time in the field under harsh conditions. With weapons, such as the AR15, you will not find a larger stockpile of ammo, spare parts, general knowledge and interchangeable components for any other weapon in the U.S. Some equipment can be significantly less expensive if you shop Army Surplus stores.

   The military is NOT the best at everything, including gear. I can use the example of backpacks. The regular issue military pack is not nearly as comfortable as a custom fit pack from a quality hiking supplier. I look first at the Military for tactics and equipment, but always see what the private sector provides as well.

vi. **Everything must work at night.** Half of the time, you are going to be in low-light conditions. Want to have some fun? Make your kids set up a tent at night. Make sure to film a video for YouTube of that one. My family is set up to drive, eat, camp and operate weapons at night. One word of warning – operating at night, in a covert way, is EXPENSIVE. This normally involves night vision or infrared (FLIR) equipment. If your location enables you to simply use candles without concern for iii above (people seeing the light), then you can avoid a large expense.

So before I add any piece of equipment, plan or action, I follow this methodology:

Will taking this step or creating this item hurt my property value? Will it do any harm?

1. Is this something I can get dual usage out of? Will it help in day-to-day life or even be useful in our Hurricane plan? Is there anyway "this" can be fun?

2. Do I need other people involved to operate or execute? Will this help me avoid other people or be more independent?

3. Can my family operate the equipment or execute the plan? Will "it" cause additional hardship? Will "it" eliminate hardship?

4. What does the military use or how do they solve "it"? How do the experts in the field do "it"?

5. Can "this" work at night? Can we "operate" it at night?

I hope all of you will perform the same tests or establish similar rules with the contents of this book. How seriously you decide to take all of its information is completely up to you and your beliefs.

Some people ask me why I plan at all if I think such events are so unlikely. I like to relate my thinking to those of household fire preparations.

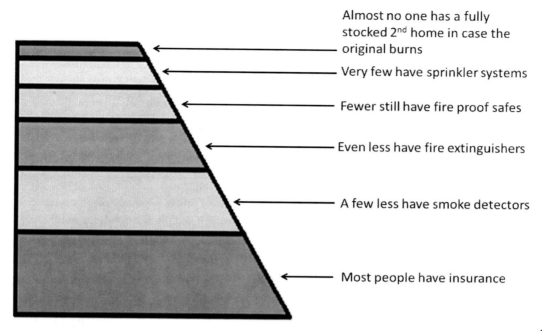

Almost no one has a fully stocked 2nd home in case the original burns

Very few have sprinkler systems

Fewer still have fire proof safes

Even less have fire extinguishers

A few less have smoke detectors

Most people have insurance

Figure 1 - Levels of Fire Preparations

Between 2005 and 2009, there was an average of 378,000 house fires each year[1]. These caused over 2,500 deaths per year.

According to the National Association of Realtors, there are approximately 80,000,000 homes in the U.S.

That means the chances of a house fire are .0047%.

Not a likely event – yet most Americans spend considerable funds – just in case. I, in relation to preparing, have fire extinguishers. You may have more or less depending on your beliefs.

---

[1] FEMA report from http://www.usfa.dhs.gov/statistics/estimates/index.shtm

3.1 Terms

*Si vis pacem, para bellum (**If you wish for peace, prepare for war**)*

- Publius Flavius Vegetius Renatus (5th Century Latin Author)

While this book is not an instruction manual for a war college or military personnel, it is not a coincidence that the people who just happen to have the most experience and expertise in defending a location are those with combat knowledge. For this reason, I use the vast wealth of knowledge available from military's experience to describe a few terms and concepts that you should understand before we begin a defensive plan.

If you don't have a military background, don't be concerned. Most of this is good old common sense. I use military-based terminology because, after you familiarize yourself with it, it provides a solid, clear definition. In reality, most of this information can be related to games we played as children. If you ever played team sports, hide-and-seek, Marco Polo or even cowboys and indians, you already instinctively know most of this.

Figure 2 - Good Old Cowboys and Indians

3.2 Types of Attack

The first terms to learn involve how someone would attack your position (location). There are three basic types of attack:

Indirect – Attack from a distance or siege. Normally, this involves placing "fire" on the target from a distance in order to destroy it or cause the defenders to abandon it. Someone shooting at you from a distance is indirect.

Frontal – If you have ever seen the old war movies where all the soldiers line up and charge the fort, this is a frontal attack. A frontal attack concentrates the attackers on a single point of the target.

Enveloping – This method was best described by General George Patton, who once said, *"Hold them by the nose and kick them in the ass."* Basically, the attacker engages the strongest point of the defense (location for our purposes) with a small force and the main attacking force maneuvers to hit the target from the side(s) or rear.

To prepare for the defense of our location, our plan needs to address all three types of attack. The likelihood of how your location would be engaged depends on several different factors that we will address in later chapters. I fear, and thus prepare for these in the following order:

I believe that an **indirect** method is the easiest of the three for the attacker. It has the least amount of risk and can actually be used to gather information (reconnaissance by fire). If our villain believes his target may be heavily defended, he may "snipe" at your location to see how you react. From a concealed position, he can be very effective and pose little risk to himself or his group.

Enveloping is my second most probable method. One of the first thoughts many people have is that an enveloping attack is too sophisticated to be performed by roving bands of scavengers or the starving. Actually, we have used enveloping tactics since we were children. If you played sports, did you ever use "head fakes"? If you watch football, most defenses use enveloping methods to "blitz" the offensive. The same can be said of the football offense performing a fake handoff before the pass. You focus the attention of your opponent elsewhere, anywhere but the primary point of attack. I have watched "rookie" paintball teams naturally fall into an enveloping attack without the slightest bit of military training, so it is likely that any disorganized band of aggressors will naturally discover the same tactics.

I believe the <u>least</u> likely method to be used against my location is a **frontal assault**. My logic for this is that our attacker does not have a political or military motivation. They, most likely, want my food, water, supplies or women (they don't know my wife). A frontal assault can be BRUTAL on the attacker from the aspect of casualties. Remember, we are defending a location after a major breakdown of society, so medical supplies and services will probably be limited.

Any injury could eventually be fatal[2] and our attackers will know this. If the attacker is merely scavenging for their own survival, they would probably "move on" to an easier target before attempting a frontal assault.

3.3 Types of Defense

We should also cover the two basic types of defense, since that is our primary purpose:

Passive Defense – The best example of a "passive" defense is camouflage. Stealth is another form of passive defense as would be "hiding in plain sight."

Active Defense – Direct action against the attacker, such as shooting at them. An active defensive strategy would also try to project power or "look big and strong." Floodlights, barbwire, stake pits and other easily visible preparations would shout out "I am too strong to attack, go elsewhere."

An ongoing debate amongst those who prepare is what type of defense will work the best. Some people believe you should make your location look like a modern day fire base with barbwire, trenches, machine gun nests and guard towers. Others believe you should hide in plain sight – make your location look as though no one is there or it has already been ransacked and looted. These two schools of thought both have merit. Both also have a long list of positives and negatives. As we fill in the variables on our worksheet, it should become apparent which strategy should perform best for you and your location.

A passive defense can be VERY effective for many situations and has the following list of positives:

- > **Less expensive** – thus more return on investment
- > **Less intrusive** - none of us KNOW that any event is going to happen or what is it going to be, or how society is going to react. For this reason, any type of defense that does not impact our daily lives and activities around our location is a good thing
- > **Less visible** to your neighbors and passersby
- > **Requires less skill** by the defenders. No offense to my alpha-male readers, but there is a high probability that most of your "defenders" will NOT be world-class warriors or even have combat experience. Using passive methods allows a longer period of time for the average person to adjust to the fear, shock, confusion and fog of war
- > **Can become active** if properly configured and planned

The Passive Defense also has its negatives:

- > Looters or roamers may be attracted to your location because it appears vacant
- > The overall offensive capabilities of a passive defense are typically less than an active
- > Hiding or "cowering in fear" does not sit well with some people

---

[2] More people die from infections and dieses in war than actual combat.

An Active Defense has the following positives:

> ➤ **Sends a strong message** – don't mess with us or you will get hurt. STAY AWAY!
> ➤ Allows for **more freedom** of movement in daily activities
> ➤ Can **withstand attacks** of larger size with more capabilities

The Drawbacks of an Active Defensive Strategy are:

> ➤ More expensive
> ➤ Requires more skills by the defenders
> ➤ Requires a greater number of defenders
> ➤ May attract the "helpless and pleading" or those desperate for any type of security
> ➤ Very difficult to become passive once implemented

We, unfortunately, will also have to address certain dark aspects of an **ANY TYPE** of defense in our plan. To avoid this topic would be foolish and naive. Let's just be clear and upfront right now – defending your location most likely means hurting, and perhaps, killing people.

Despite what you may have seen on TV, or in movies, **taking a human life is difficult**. Even the most hardcore warriors worried about how they would react in their first combat. Will I run? Will I be able to pull the trigger? Will I be able to KILL? It is a little known fact that during the Civil War, the Union Army found that a large percentage of the soldiers, while on the skirmish line, were NOT firing at the enemy. The studies found that their weapons were "double loaded", which meant they did **not** "fire", and then reloaded when ordered (a much more visible activity). One rifle had over 20 "balls" loaded in it. Col. David Grossman[3], U.S. Army (Ret.) included extensive research on this topic in his book *ON KILLING*. He quoted various studies that showed the average firing rate – the percentage of front line troops who actually fired their weapons – was only 15% to 20%. Repetitive training methods brought the firing rate up to about 55% in Korea and 90% to 95% in Vietnam.

This information alone should be enough to convince even the most aggressive individuals to consider a passive strategy as the initial plan. Even if your mindset can accept the "it's me or them" concept, you will probably not be alone during defensive actions. Family members, friends and relatives may be there and to believe everyone will have the same mindset about killing is wishful thinking at best.

There is, however, a strong argument to be made for an active defense right from the start. If your group is big enough and your supplies are deep enough, this may be a wise strategy. The concept of projecting "we are loud and proud – if you mess with us, we are going to kick your sorry butt" has some attractive, logical qualities.

Most of the people who believe in an initial active stance are part of a large, well organized group. They have a command and control hierarchy in place and are already organized. While I have not found this

---

[3] You can read more on Col. Grossman's excellent work at www.killology.com

situation to be common among preppers, the subject is worth exploring for our purposes. If you are part of this smaller group of readers, you will still find value here.

My primary issue with an active posture is that the typical American family unit, group or team will not have a large pool of well-trained, disciplined fighters at their disposal. I believe that just plain old surviving is going to take the majority of everyone's time and the more I have to keep watch, the less time I have to gather food.

So while I have found that a passive defense is the best plan for most situations this book will address both methods in detail so that you can make the best decisions for your circumstances.

3.4 Other Terms and Concepts

There are seven basic terms, which describe actions and concepts we need to cover. These should be understood as they apply to any method of defense.

Key Placement of Weapons Systems – An active defense will almost certainly require shooting at attackers. Where you put your weapons or fighting positions can make all the difference. In the following chapters we will go into detail about this.

Pre-Position – One of the advantages of a fixed location is that the defenders (you) can pre-stock or pre-position supplies such as water, ammunition, medical supplies and food. The attackers have to basically carry all they need on their backs.

Multiple Angles of Fire – Attackers have an advantage in that their focus is convergent, while your focus has to be divergent. You, as the defender, have to pay attention for up to 360 degrees of your position while the attacker only has to focus on the area directly in front of him. But, what if you could cause the attacker to "worry" about more than one angle? The attacker would then have to divide his forces or adjust his objectives and that would weaken him.

Spoiler Attacks – Your attackers have a number of problems. There will be phases of the attack when they and their plan are vulnerable. History is full of examples where a well-timed action by the defenders has "spoiled" the entire attack. During the American Revolution, the "rebels" started using sharp shooters to target those bright, shiny British Officers riding around on their horses. As the officers were gathering their troops for an attack, shouting orders and riding up and down the line, a single well placed shot would disrupt the entire British effort. This is a very simple, but effective example of a "spoiler" attack.

Fallback or Egress – You may not be able to hold your location. How are you going to get out? Last stands, defense to the last man and all of those Hollywood romantic concepts aside, the reality is you may have to bug out. Maybe the scavengers take what they can carry and then leave? Living to fight another day is the top priority. There is no dishonor in a fighting retreat.

Area Denial Systems (ADS) – This term is exactly what it says – having an area, like a corner of your location that is denied to the attackers. In the military realm, an example of an Area Denial System would be a mine field. Any approach you can "take away" from the attacker is to your advantage.

Early Warning Systems (EWS) – The absolute worst case for any defender is to be surprised. We will cover various techniques that will allow you to sleep well at night and not worry about any wolves being at the door before you know it.

All of the above terms and concepts will be detailed in later sections and rated on your worksheet. While these items may sound very military in nature, they are really quite practical and easy to understand. In addition, they are important for several reasons that you probably have not considered. Let's explore pre-positioning, as an example.

I have always found it ironic that some preppers can invest in huge inventories of ammunition, food, and medical supplies, but give little thought to pre-positioning those valuable commodities.

Even if you take fire, theft and storage space out of the equation, keeping all of your important survival items in one place makes no sense. Let's take a very simple test to see why this is important.

Pretend you heard a post-TEOTWAWKI sound outside. You want walk around your house, on "patrol" with the following items:

- Rifle and Secondary Weapon (pistol)
- Ammunition - A couple of spare magazines/clips for each weapon
- Water & Snack
- Binoculars & Flashlight
- Glasses (not for protection if you gun blows up) & ear plugs

Can you keep your rifle up and ready like it should be?

Can you get to your secondary quickly or does your rifle sling get in the way?

Can you take a drink without setting the rifle down?

Can you view through the binoculars without tangling your rifle sling?

Can you go prone or take a knee without setting your equipment aside?

If you think I am splitting hairs here – **try it for an hour or two.** This is a VERY basic load to carry, yet you will find it is a pain if you don't have the right equipment (load vest) or have these items pre-positioned in a few key spots. Pre-positioning makes sense. Why not pre-position a small box with these items at every corner of your house? That way you only have to carry the rifle and pistol and can move around freely.

4. The Event Horizon

Before any plans can be made concerning security, it is important to decide upon a timeline or the "Event Horizon" as it might be called.

Social Behavioral Sciences are quite advanced in this area. Volumes have been written about how people react when faced with uncertainty or challenges that threaten their daily life or existence. While no two humans are exactly alike, empirical evidence provides for several cardinalities that we can use for preparations. For example, throughout the history of mankind, we have always re-grouped and organized regardless of the change to our environment. We, with the exception of sociopaths, are social creatures and need other humans. Here are some basic premises that we can utilize as a foundation for our security plans:

- Humans will eventually group together. Even in the Dark Ages, villages, towns, and eventually city-states formed, organized and propagated.
- Humans, over the long term, need interaction with other humans. The mountain men of early America grouped together for annual events and were happy when they came across one another in the wild.
- Throughout history, even the "outlaws", the most anti-social of humans, grouped together in "gangs."
- The exchange of goods or services will occur, regardless of the level of government or security. None of us is an expert on all things required for life (division of labor). We may be able to "get by" for periods of time, but each has certain areas of expertise that improves the quality of life over the long term. You may be able to grow food, while I can make a great pair of leather boots and eventually, we will meet and trade.
- Out of any group, a hierarchy or organization will form. In early mankind, it is believed that leadership was determined by the most physically powerful. Native American Tribes tended to have leadership based on age, wisdom and experience. Spiritual leadership (medicine men or the Catholic Church) has always played a role, especially in the Dark Ages. There is no way to predict future events, but for the purposes of our planning, it is enough to know that some sort of leadership and organization will evolve out of the ashes.

If you take the basics of Human Social Behavior you can calculate a time-line critical for your security preparation.

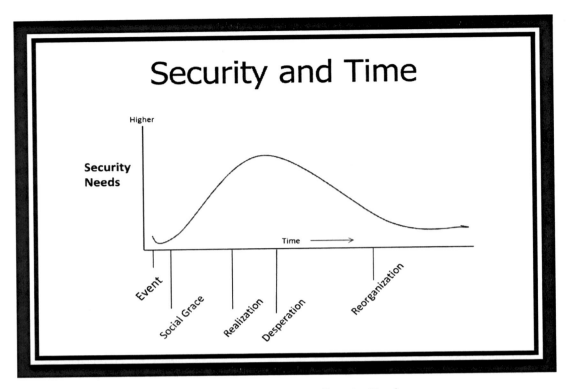

Figure 3 - Time vs. Security Needs

Event – The trigger or act that initializes your plan. This could be practically anything, such as an approaching storm, a terrorist attack or even the outbreak of war.

Social Grace – Historically, when an "event" has occurred, people have initially banded together to help one another. I call this the *Grace Period* and the duration is directly related to the severity of the event. As an example, shortly after Hurricane Rita in Houston, the electrical power was out for most of the city. It is well documented that people who had generators would commonly offer to store the frozen food for neighbors who did not have electricity. People shared and helped one another.

Realization – When a severe event occurs, Realization will set in. People will become more "self-centered" or independent. During Katrina, this is the stage that general looting began.

Desperation – Again, depending on the severity of the event, desperation will set in when basic services, security or other needs are not available. The Super Dome in New Orleans after Katrina is a prime example. While initial news reports of murder, rape and other "bad" behavior were greatly exaggerated, the more time that expired, the more desperate those people became.

Reorganization – At some point, humans will organize. We always have. The amount of time that expires between Desperation and Reorganization will depend on the severity of the event. This means that you can establish parameters within your plan. You will not be on "Red Alert" forever and that is important to know.

In summary, our plan does not have to be infinite in duration. After some time, we will organize and share the burdens. This is important for several reasons, not the least of which is morale. If the unlikely happens, there is hope that life will get back to "normal" at some point in time in the future.

Another reason why this is important to understand, and believe, is our equipment does not have to last forever. This takes a lot of stress out of our plan. I can most likely stock up enough ammunition to make it through, so I don't have to learn how to make arrows for my bow. A single rifle, with one as a spare, will suffice. I will probably not need three or more rifles to last my decedents for the next 300 years.

4.1 The Event

"The Event" is probably the most unknown, unpredictable variable in any defense scenario. Many preparedness experts attempt to classify the "event" into levels of severity, duration, warning periods and triggers. Of course, like any futuristic planning exercise, one can quickly find an exception to any classification. In military terminology, the battle plan falls apart at the first shot, and with any plan based solely on the classification of "events", the first shot does not even have to be fired to find issues with it. We will use a different method to produce a flexible plan so that you can adapt quickly and prevail.

4.1.1 Warnings

History tells us that with the exception of a natural disaster, you will actually have some time before you have to implement your plan. Short of a hurricane, earth quake, flood or tornado, you will have trouble finding any historical event that happened "overnight" or without some period of warning:

- During the economic collapse of the Great Depression, it took weeks before desperation set in.
- While the assassination of Dr. Martin Luther King (April 4th) prompted riots in several large American cities, it was a few days after that horrible event before the violence began.

Therefore you will have some amount of time to implement your plan. This should not be viewed as an excuse not to prepare. Anyone who lives along the Gulf Coast can tell you – don't try to buy plywood at Home Depot after the storm is predicted to hit your area. The message is to have your plywood in the garage and you will have time to install it.

I know this goes against the advice of several "survival experts" who claim you will not have any warning. I just can't see a single example in our history where this has been the case. The United States Government is not going to fall overnight.

You should still prepare, because events can impact the availability of some of the equipment and supplies required for any defense. When President Obama was elected, there was a rush to purchase assault weapons. Everyone was convinced he was going to ban this type of firearm. At a gun show, I saw a dealer with a picture of the President claiming he was the "Sales Person of the Year". Prices went up and availability was an issue for several different models.

Recently, there was a shortage of ammunition in the U.S. While there were several rumors about the reasons why, the bottom line is there was a shortage. No event occurred or was reported, yet I felt sorry for anyone who was trying to stock up. The point being that you should not wait to prepare, but you will have time to implement.

4.1.2 Scale

Of all of the variables, I believe the scale of the "event" is the most critical for any plan. The scale you want to plan for will impact it more than any other single variable. The larger the scale you believe is likely, or within your capabilities, the more it will cost to prepare for.

For the purposes of your plan, you need to classify scale into one of three categories:

1. Localized
2. Regionalized
3. National

If the event is **local**, such as a tornado, your plan does not have to be as robust. Eventually, help will be on the way. Within 1-3 days, you can expect first responders, some level of security, and probably the basic establishment of services (Red Cross shelters at worst).

If the event is **regional**, your plan must be slightly more robust. An earthquake or large hurricane would be an example. A regional event, while more serious, has not historically justified the implementation of a full defensive plan. Even with Katrina impacting four states, there were not wide-spread security issues, looting or lawlessness. While it is true that isolated areas, such as New Orleans did experience looting, it was primarily for monetary gain, not starving masses raiding houses looking for food. Security in a regional event should be taken seriously, but the level of protection required is significantly less than full blown anarchy.

A **national** event is the biggest concern. An economic breakdown, EMP attack or other action that impacts the entire country is what most of us really plan for. A national event means that police, fire and medical services could eventually disappear. Food distribution, electrical power, gasoline and other basic necessities will not be available. Hope disappears for many, and desperation sets in. There are very few scenarios where a national event happens immediately. Even an EMP attack or pandemic, about the most dangerous events I can visualize, will not eliminate our entire infrastructure overnight.

As the event goes from local to national, the extent of your preparations has to increase. It is up to you to determine what you believe is realistic or likely, and what is not. I, for example, do not believe an EMP[4] attack would disable as much infrastructure as others believe. My truck, surge protected computer and other electronic devices can survive lightning strikes, which carry about 1,000,000 times the energy of an EMP wave. I researched the use of Faraday cages, grounding systems and other precautions extensively and reached my conclusion. You may reach a different conclusion and that is why your beliefs are so important in the scope of your plan.

One should **not** assume that the scale of an event will remain constant. For example, if Southern California had a major earthquake right after Katrina and shortly thereafter a major terrorist attack had occurred, the capability of the United States to react and recover economically would have been greatly threatened.

---

[4] The Starfish Prime weapons testing in July 1962, which shorted street lights in Hawaii and caused other minor damage, made the public aware of the potential danger of EMP.

4.2 The Enemy

Know thy self, Know thy enemy – Sun Tzu, The Art of War, 500BC

While "Know thy enemy" is a concept that may sound logical, for our purposes, it can be difficult to encompass in a security plan. For an army, preparing to fight a finite list of potential foes, intelligence gathering and subsequent planning for that enemy is an ongoing process.

For our purposes, we don't know very much about who we might have to defend against – because they don't exist yet. History can tell us certain facts, which for our purposes have a high probability of being true, but no one REALLY knows.

It is commonly known that malnutrition causes psychosis, agitation and aggression in human beings. Hungry people will do unthinkable things and most likely, they will be the Enemy.

What we can be sure of is that given our Event Horizon (Figure 3), the threat will change as time progresses. For our planning purposes, we should assume that the enemy will become more of a serious threat as time goes by during the phase of Desperation. It is also a safe assumption that the capabilities of any potential foe will follow the same bell curve as the Event Horizon shown previously. Given the eventual depletion of supplies, such as batteries, ammunition, medical goods and mobility, the strength of any potential attacker will decline over time.

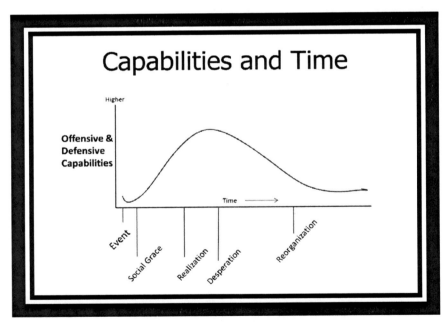

Figure 4 - Capabilities of Both Defense and Potential Foes

The same curve can be used to describe YOUR defensive capabilities. Unless the location you plan on defending has infinite supplies and you are immortal, your defensive capabilities will decline over time as well.

One of the most interesting prepper plans I have ever heard involved a group of local neighbors who had plans to "take and hold" a Wal-Mart distribution center near their small town. A few of them worked at the facility and they had detailed drawings and preparations ready. They believed that with virtually unlimited food, supplies, ammo and medicine they could organize and control the local area for months, perhaps even years. The running joke was that they would be the "Warlords of the Wal-Mart." They, however, started in-fighting over distribution. It seemed that part of the group wanted to keep it all to themselves and their families, while others believed they should use their "gold mine" to organize and control the surrounding area. It probably didn't help when someone pointed out that EVERYONE in town knew it was there, and would probably have the idea to go "loot" the place. Would they, holding the facility, be able to harm or turn away the people they had grown up with and known all their lives? **This gives an entirely new perspective to "Know thy enemy."**

Assumptions we can make about our potential attackers are based on historical examples:

1. Initial organizations, or groups, will have a small number of members. There is a school of thought amongst those who study Social Sciences about Organization and Leadership, which concludes that most early formation leadership will be challenged and splintering will occur. This means that the number of people in any single group will reach a certain size and then a separation or division will ensue. We have all seen this with churches, clubs, peer groups and even sports leagues. At some point, someone will disagree and challenge the leadership or believe their way is the better way and splinter off. A certain number of members will follow them. As desperation sets in, success will cause a decline in challenges. Everyone likes a winner so some groups will eventually grow in size.
2. Non-governmental organizations, such as churches, motorcycle clubs, street gangs and drug cartels will be the first to take action as independent groups.
3. Mobility will be a key factor in their capabilities. Regardless of horses, trucks, motorcycles or bicycles, a mobile threat is a more potent threat.
4. Security will be the initial draw or attraction of any group. Street gangs recruit members because of security or "being safe" in the neighborhood. This translates into the potential for the most aggressive to become the largest.

Even in complete anarchy, people will organize into groups. These groups will be aggressive if not outright violent. They will provide security through strength and will deliver essentials, by any method, for their members. The good news is that they will likely be initially small in number. The bad news is that as time goes by their size will increase and become more effective.

Our purpose is to defend a location. Again, historical examples can give us some indication of how we should structure our defensive plan against this undefined foe. Until recently, a fixed location has always had the advantage over an attacking enemy. For thousands of years, people have built castles, forts, bases and other fixed structures for the purpose of security. From a military perspective, they were successful and only with the advent of modern air power and the long range projection of power (missiles and modern artillery) did they become obsolete. Currently, from a military perspective, if it is FIXED, it is DEAD.

We, however, are not planning on fighting a modern military (if you are – you're reading the wrong book). Our attackers will not have air power or missiles. While long range rifles can project power over great distance, their tactical impact is limited. That means any attacking force needs to outnumber the defenders of a fixed position by a large margin. Our potential attackers should not have numbers, so our decision to defend a fixed location is valid. The following table shows the advantages and disadvantages for any force attacking a fixed, defended location:

Factor	Advantage	Notes
Supplies	Fixed Location	A mobile force can only carry so much ammunition, food and water with them. A fixed location should have more supplies.
Cover	Fixed Location	A properly configured location will have more effective cover than the area surrounding it (fields of fire). Any approach should be exposed.
Facilities	Fixed Location	Shelter, heat, and operational areas all should be superior for the castle vs. the sieging force.
Accuracy of Projection	Fixed Location	If I am stationary, I can shoot more accurately than if I am charging the fort.
Point of Attack	Attacker	A defensive position has to cover 360 degrees. An attacker knows where the defender is.
Initiative	Attacker	The attacker decides when to "charge". The defender has to wait for the attack.
Converging Fire	Attacker	A defender's fire is diverging.

Figure 5 - Advantages and Disadvantages of a Fixed Location

4.3 What will the Government do?

The concept of a "complete" break-down in society is unlikely. It has never happened in recent history, despite such horrific events such as the Great Depression or the Civil War. What is more likely is that some form of government control will exist in the major cities or population centers. This, from a military perspective, is predictable.

In several past and present conflicts, such as Vietnam, Iraq and Afghanistan (both the USSR and NATO), the military has elected to occupy and control the cities. The country side was a secondary priority, and thus became the "Wild West."

If you will recall, after Iraq fell in the 2nd Gulf War, there was widespread looting in Baghdad, even at museums and governmental locations. The Army, being completely unprepared for that scenario, resorted to marshal law and concentrated its forces in the major cities.

The same can be said of the South after the Civil War. The Union established control of the major cities first. The country was a wild and dangerous place for a considerable period of time.

Put yourself in the military's shoes – your mission is to maintain order and ensure the survival of as many citizens as possible. Since even the U.S. Military has limited resources, that means you have to utilize your resources where they will have the best chance of accomplishing your mission. That means the cities.

Bugging Out to the cities may be a valid option for some people. If you have the capability to get there and you don't mind living like the New Orleans evacuees did in the Houston[5] Astrodome, it would probably be an option worth serious consideration. Since you have purchased this book, I assume you are thinking more like I am – that would be the last option for my family.

Some experts believe that select local governments will be quick to react and organize. There have been documentaries made that depict the local sheriff or police departments taking control and organizing small towns. For some locations, this may be realistic.

4.4 Living by the Gun

I attend shooting events, classes and competitions regularly. It is common for the topic of "end times", SHTF (*Shit Hits The Fan*), or TEOTWAWKI (*The End Of The World As We Know It*) to come up during breaks or after hours. One of the most common phrases you will hear is "the zombie wars", which to some, is actually a metaphor for "if I have to shoot large numbers of my fellow humans – who no longer act like humans." The phrase is more polite in civilized company than saying "when I may have to gun down hoards of my fellow citizens." You would be pressed to find a single one of them who actually believes that the dead will rise and need to be "taken care of."

The attendees at these events are typically very hardcore professional people who carry a weapon as part of their job. It is not unusual to find yourself in the company of active military, law enforcement, SWAT, ex-military or just plain old anarchists (normally not welcome, so they try and hide it).

I think the average person would be shocked to know the underlying thought process of some of these professionals. When their "on duty" guard is let down, and they feel comfortable around the "camp fire", how they think and what their plans are is not a pretty picture for the average prepper.

An all too common philosophy concerning post-event planning is:

---

[5] I mean zero negativity towards the people of Houston and how they treated those brought in from New Orleans. It was a well-organized, charitable effort of heroic proportions. It remains a well-deserved point of pride for the people of that city and the state of Texas.

If I have enough weapons, skills and ammunition, I can take everything else I need.

You have to admit, the concept may have romantic qualities for some people. Younger men without families who still believe they are invincible or who have survived the harsh conditions of war may not properly think through the consequences. I think some even envision themselves as roaming the Old West, living off the land.

The concept of preparing may be beyond their capabilities, both financial and physical. It is a lot easier to obtain a good weapon and store a lot of ammunition than it is to acquire months of food and water, a generator and all of the other items preppers stock up on.

It is an easy way out, both physically and mentally.

These are the people I fear most in a post-event world. They are trained, used to violence and will attract recruits easily. They are comfortable with a command and control structure and will naturally be attracted to the initial organizations being formed. They may even lead them.

If you think I am being a fear monger or exaggerating the situation, I need to confess that I, for years, was someone who planned to "live by the gun" if it all went to hell.

I was a teenager in the 1970's. Back in the day, most of us were convinced that a nuclear war was a real possibility. The USSR (better dead than red) and the United States were on the brink of deciding "who was the biggest kid on the block" by throwing hot, hydrogen punches at each other, or so it seemed.

When I was 14, the local Sunday paper published an article about the effects of a nuclear attack. It showed a diagram of the city center with rings drawn depicting the damage at various distances from ground zero. It ranged from being vaporized instantly to describing the blind masses stumbling around the ruble while their blistered skin peeled off. That damn thing kept me up at night for at least a week.

I bet a lot of you remember the 1983 TV movie called *THE DAY AFTER*. I was in my early 20's when it aired, and I still have images from that show in my mind. It was, at that time, one of the most watched TV events ever, with some estimations being that **HALF** of the adult population were viewers.

I grew up with the mindset that the "last war" would occur and civilization would completely break down. I, as a young man with limited resources, always believed that my skills with a weapon would get me through.

For some years, as I moved around the country taking different jobs, I would make mental notes about my location. How fast can I get to the nearest K-Mart (big chain store back in the pre-Wal-Mart days) and grocery store? Where is the local fuel distribution company located? How strong is their fence?

It was not unusual for my shooting buddies and me to have conversations along the lines of:

ME: Where are you going if they send up the balloon (term used to describe nuclear war)?

BUDDY: My cousin has a place out in the country. There is a sporting goods store that has lots of ammo down the road from my apartment. There are only a couple of old ladies working in there during the day. I figure I will stop in and help myself to all the ammo I can carry, grab a new sleeping bag on the way out and head to my cousin's place. What about you?

ME: Where is that store?

My emergency kit, for years, contained a .45 ACP pistol, an M1 carbine rifle, a few boxes of shells and bolt cutters. As I befriended co-workers, attended social events and dated various young ladies, I always made mental notes about neighborhoods, specific features and other items that would benefit me if the "end times" occurred.

I remember picking up a nice young lady for a date at her parent's home. Her mother was canning from the garden. I thought "how interesting" as I took the tour of their basement storage area. "My mother grew up in the Great Depression and taught me to can. It saves us money and we can eat well for months with what I get from the garden," she said. My thoughts were along the lines of "what a great place to be if it all goes to hell", not "I should learn to can food – this is a great idea."

It is important to understand this mindset, because these are the people who will most likely be a problem in a post-event world.

When there is no longer a concern of punishment from the law, things change dramatically. Every survival expert will tell you - when the hunger in your belly becomes unbearable, you will eat and do things you thought were unimaginable before.

So, while we are on the topic of unimaginable, put yourself in the mind of the bad guy. Please keep in mind, the following is meant to make you think and recognize potential dangers – not something I personally would EVER consider.

If someone is "living by the gun", here are some examples of how they might think and operate:

- Use high places (trees, buildings, and towers) to observe and locate light, sounds or smells.
- Scout any potential source first. Observe and note any activity. Information is power.
- An unoccupied location is always better than an occupied one, but an occupied place probably has what you need. Unoccupied locations of value will become scarce as scavenging occurs.
- Always approach and attempt to beg or barter. At worst, it can provide you with more information in case you have to come back in the middle of the night.
- Try to steal if beg/barter fails. They probably have more than what they need anyway.
- Kidnapping is better than fighting. Take a kid, let them know you have the kid and exchange the kid for what you want. A woman works as well.
- If no other option exists but to "take" what you need, which means fighting, do so from a distance. Sniping is safer than walking up and kicking in the door.
- If sniping is not an option, then IT IS ON. Hit them and hit them as hard as you can. Shock and awe. They will probably run when the shooting starts. If not, you are already committed by then.
- You would prefer to be on a team or in a group. There is just too much to worry about being alone and four of five can be more effective. Safety in numbers.

Now I consider myself a man of principle and character. While the concept is completely disgusting to me, I do believe it is realistic to prepare for people with this mindset. If you look at Somalia, the above method of operation is common. Think about pirates in the headlines.

You can also study guerrilla warfare over the ages. The Viet Cong did not live off of the land – they took what they needed from villages. In Iraq, the insurgents initially had support from the tribes. When that support faltered, they attempted to take what they needed by force. That was the turning point in the war because the tribes came to the U.S. Army for protection. In a post-event world, there may not be a U.S. Army to turn to.

5. The Location

I will refer to the place we plan to defend, the place where we will be staying as "the location." The location can be a home, campground, cave, your girlfriend's house or an underground bunker. It is where you will hang your hat. We have to define our location in some unusual ways because every place is different. A remote farm requires a different plan from a high rise condo. A mobile camper requires a temporary, reproducible preparation when compared to a fixed location.

Some people plan to "bug out" while others plan to "bug in", or remain in their primary domain. Still others plan on a mobile (camper or RV) type of existence. Regardless of what your plan is, you will still have to be ready to defend wherever you lay your head at night.

According to the U.S. Census Bureau, 14% of Americans live in apartment buildings. Planning for the defense of that type of location is really not much different from a standalone home. The primary issue most apartment dwellers face is storage space. Stocking up on supplies takes a large amount of space. When I talk to apartment dwellers about serious preparations, the conversation eventually ends up with a bug-out plan. An apartment or condo is defendable with preparation and clever thinking.

A high rise apartment is probably the easiest location you can think of to defend short of a Taliban cave. Concrete and steel structure, good visibility and limited access make the concept very appealing initially. Again, the problem is storage. The lack of egress options (escape) and the fact that you will have great leg conditioning from going up and down flights of stairs without an elevator (no electricity) aside, how are you going to store the food, water, and other essentials required for the long term? How are you going to resupply? We will also address the defense of a high rise unit.

Some people have basements or a subterranean BOL (Bug Out Location). Personally, I have never liked this type of shelter for defensive purposes unless we are talking about a nuclear fallout event. For just about every other type of event, it would not be my first choice. If you have chosen a below ground location because you believe it will be easier to defend, I hope this book causes you to reconsider.

As most veterans of the Vietnam War will tell you, subterranean locations can be VERY effective. Being experts at tunneling, the North Vietnamese Army (and the Viet Cong) built entire bases beneath the surface of the earth. They had to be, because of vastly superior American fire power. A below-ground location solves a lot of problems associated with defense if configured properly. If you have the manpower, resources, and the type of soil that supports tunneling or below ground locations, you may be well ahead of the curve.

I have never considered a subterranean location because of several drawbacks, including the fact that my area of the world does not have the right soil for tunneling.

The typical basement is similar to a cave in that it has a single way in or out. I think this is a very bad idea. Unless you have an escape tunnel (egress), your options in a basement are limited if you are faced with an overwhelming force. One smoke grenade, let alone a quart of gasoline, glass bottle and a rag can end a basement defense in a few minutes.

Basements also offer a very poor observation capability. One important aspect of an effective defense is the ability to spot the attackers at a distance. This is hard to do from ground level or lower.

However, my main problem with basements, root cellars, and tunnels is the mental effects of living that way. All of us plan, prepare, spend, and ponder in order to continue life. For me, that means being outside and having a somewhat productive existence. I hope the vast majority of my days would be spent teaching my children the skills to continue growing and gathering food and eventually playing a role in the rebuilding of our society. All of these are more difficult to do if you are hiding in a tunnel.

For years, Osama bin Laden was thought to be hiding in a cave. As it turns out, he was hiding in plain sight and not in a remote, subterranean fortress. We will probably never know why a man being hunted by the most powerful military in the world decided on a more exposed, open BOL as opposed to a cave. Could it be that the cave was too restrictive or felt like being in prison?

As you read through this book, it does not address caves or sub-terrain locations. While the rules are all basically the same, those locations are rare. I have not diagramed examples nor do I spend a lot of time with them.

Overall, there are four initial factors to consider when performing an analysis of any location to be defended:

- Population Density of the surrounding areas
- Proximity to major roadways
- Physical Area – to be defended
- Visibility

The following sections will provide instruction and examples so that you can fill in the values on the worksheet and begin the evaluation.

5.1 Population Density

The Population Density of surrounding areas can be easily determined from the internet. If you can find the location you want to defend on a map, you can see how many people are in the general area. As stated in Chapter 3, Methodology, in a breakdown, PEOPLE will be the biggest single problem. We are, after all, creating a defensive plan against people, not roaming packs of dogs or feral hogs. For the United States, Wikipedia is a simple, free source of Population Density Maps like the one for Texas below.

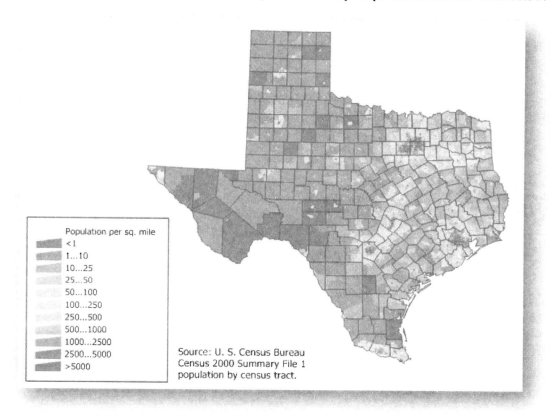

Population per sq. mile
< 1
1...10
10...25
25...50
50...100
100...250
250...500
500...1000
1000...2500
2500...5000
>5000

Source: U. S. Census Bureau
Census 2000 Summary File 1
population by census tract.

Figure 6 - Population Density Map of Texas

If you live outside of the United States, you can still find free maps for most locations on the net, but you may have to do a little searching. For our formula, you need to find the location you want to defend (Bug In or Bug Out) and enter the population per square mile in the worksheet cell for Population Density.

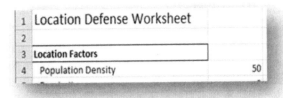

1	Location Defense Worksheet	
2		
3	**Location Factors**	
4	Population Density	50

5.2 Proximity Factor

The Proximity Factor is a count of how many roadways or evacuation routes your location is "close" to. A simple gas station folder map can be used. Just draw a straight line (as the crow flies) between your location and the nearest major interstate or highway. I use a rule of thumb of 15 miles away. Add one to your count for every major roadway within 15 miles.

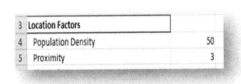

3	Location Factors	
4	Population Density	50
5	Proximity	3

YOU SHOULD ENTER YOUR VALUE IN THE WORKSHEET CELL LABELED PROXIMITY. THE NUMBER 3 IS SHOWN IN THE EXAMPLE.

Why is this important? During the evacuation of Houston for Hurricane Rita, every major roadway surrounding Houston was clogged with standstill traffic for days. The people living in low-population areas, over 100 miles outside of the city, suddenly had a lot of "new friends" using their streets, gas stations, hotels and yards. The swarm of Houston locusts descended upon them in biblical proportions and to this day, you can hear local residents telling stories about it.

While very little crime arose out of that situation, one can only speculate if that would have been the case given a more permanent event. The situation, if the event causing the exodus had been something more national, may have gotten out of control. Most of the people stuck in that mess (I was one of them) were in fair spirits despite the situation. Most knew it was temporary and the worst case was their homes would suffer storm damage. That same situation, driven by an event that damaged "hope", could have been a real powder keg.

If the event we are planning for allows people to flee the big cities, they probably will. Your location may be in a very low density area and miles from the nearest large city, but if you are close to a major interstate or highway, your location may experience an overnight population explosion.

5.3 Physical Area

The Physical Area is defined as the size of the area you plan to defend. This is typically more than just the area of your home or shelter. The number should include any outdoor areas you wish to use during normal activities. I have met many people who just think of defending their homes, but this is a mistake. Unless there is a threat of fallout or other significant reason NOT to go outside, you will probably need to, if for no other reason than to avoid cabin fever.

- Do you have a garden out back?
- Do you have a swimming pool full of water?
- Do you have a barn with livestock?
- Do you have a root cellar where food is stored?
- Is there an apple tree in the front yard you plan to use?

The point being that any area you will be accessing during normal activities should be included in your definition of the Location Area. I would NOT include any areas your plan has for hunting, trapping or general scavenging. Those, one could assume, would be occasional activities where you would be more alert.

I measure the Location Area with a simple estimate of square yards (or meters). This does not have to be an exact measurement, but a close estimate. If you have no clue, then walk the area off in large steps and multiple the width times the length. *Hint: an acre has 4840 square yards.*

ENTER THE NUMBER OF SQUARE YARDS (OR METERS) IN THE WORKSHEET CELL LABELED PHYSICAL AREA. THE EXAMPLE SHOWS 2,500 AS THE VALUE.

5.4 Visibility Factor

The Visibility Factor is how "visible" your location is to surrounding areas. To determine this factor, you will need a pencil and a piece of paper in addition to the worksheet.

First off, we have to consider our Location Area. When determining the Visibility Factor, we have to include all of our Location Area. Of all our variables, this is probably the most difficult to accurately define. If your location is on a 50,000 acre desert ranch, with no visibility from the nearest country road, then your visibility rating is low. If your home is on the highest mountain side within 200 miles, then it probably can been seen by anyone in the area, especially at night.

If your location is several hundred yards off a remote country road surrounded by heavy woods, your visibility rating is also very low.

If your location borders on an interstate highway, with only a privacy fence separating you from thousands of daily passersby, then your visibility rating is very high.

I have compiled the following guide to help you determine a Visibility Factor for your location. To begin with, think about your location and the various directions it can be approached from either vehicle or on foot. If your location is on a river, then you can eliminate that direction. If a large cliff borders one side of your location, you can eliminate that one as well. A thick woods or forest reduces visibility as well.

Description	Value	Notes
A. Can be easily seen from x number of roads		Where x is the number of roads
B. Can easily be seen from x number of directions		Four points of the compass is good enough
C. Can easily be seen from x number of yards		Greatest distance of any direction

Figure 7 - Calculating for Visibility

Once you fill in the values above, do this simple equation with the values: **(A + B) x C = Visibility Factor** Let's take some examples to make sure we have an accurate visibility factor.

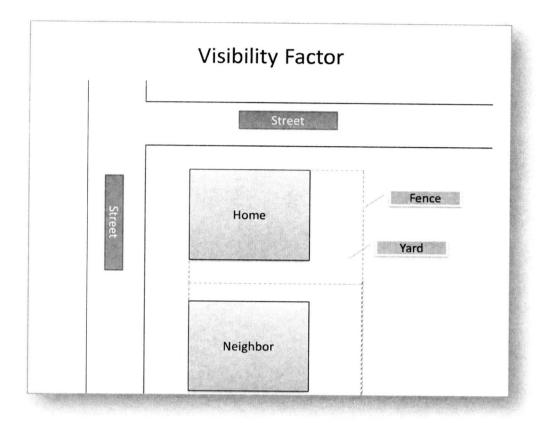

Figure 8 - Suburban Layout for Visibility

Your location is a suburban home in one of the thousands of typical neighborhoods that make up our great nation. It is on a street corner, quarter acre lot with a privacy fence around the back yard. Your visibility factor would be calculated as follows:

- Number of Roads = 2
- Number of Directions = 2
- Number of yards = 300 (straight street in front)

Our factor would be 1200, or (2+2) x 300.

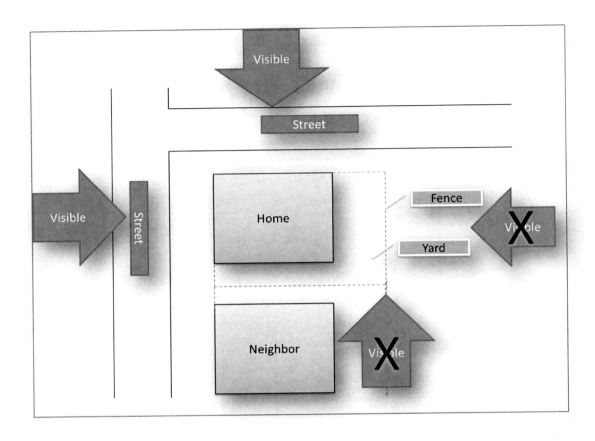

Figure 9 - Visible Directions (2) Noted by Arrows

Example II: Your location is a remote farm house on a country road in front. It is surrounded by heavy woods on two sides with a large field on the third. Your visibility factor would be calculated as follows:

- Number of Roads = 1
- Number of Directions = 2
- Number of yards = 1,500 (from the field)

Our factor would be 4,500, or (1+2) x 1500.

Example III:

Your location is a home in a wooded valley. The home is not visible from the road, and the 1 acre yard is completely surrounded by forest and hills. Your visibility factor would be calculated as follows:

- Number of Roads = 0
- Number of Directions = 0
- Number of Yards = 50

Our factor would be 0, (0 + 0) x 50.

1	Location Defense Worksheet	
2		
3	**Location Factors**	
4	Population Density	50
5	Proximity	3
6	Physical Area	2,500
7	Visibility	4880

ENTER YOUR LOCATION'S VISIBILITY FACTOR IN THE WORKSHEET CELL LABELED "VISIBILITY". THE EXAMPLE SHOWS A VALUE OF 4880.

5.5 The High Ground

High Ground is a factor to determine if your location has height or commands a solid view of the surrounding area. A two story house is an asset. A three story barn is a better asset. Rank your "view" of the area around your location on a scale of 1 to 5, with 1 being poor to 5 being "commanding."

1	Location Defense Worksheet	
2		
3	**Location Factors**	
4	Population Density	50
5	Proximity	3
6	Physical Area	2,500
7	Visibility	4880
8	High Ground	5

ENTER YOUR FACTOR IN THE WORKSHEET CELL LABELED "HIGH GROUND". THE EXAMPLE SHOWS A VALUE OF 5.

5.6 Positions and Angles

Positions and Angles is a count of the actual defensive positions available for the location and area. An example here would be a farm house with a good barn close by would be two positions. Another example would be a home with a close guest house – again, two positions.

This count should **not** include fighting positions[6], which are covered in a later section (6.12).

5.7 Open Access

Open Access is a simple count of the number of compass directions (North, South, East and West) where there are no barriers whatsoever. A wheat field would be a good example of completely open access.

- o Typical wire fences should not be counted as a limiting access.
- o Lightly wooded areas don't limit access either.

5.8 Limited Access

Limited Access is the count of the directions that are blocked by something. A privacy fence, heavy woods or other barrier that limits someone from approaching your location from that direction should be counted here.

5.9 No Access

Any barrier at your location that blocks access completely should be counted as No Access. An example would be a steep cliff face or deep river. A large pond or lake should also be counted. *While boats are common, the typical bad guy will NOT want to attempt a water crossing.*

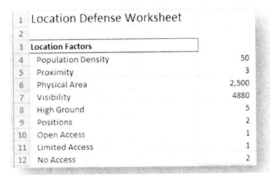

1	Location Defense Worksheet	
2		
3	**Location Factors**	
4	Population Density	50
5	Proximity	3
6	Physical Area	2,500
7	Visibility	4880
8	High Ground	5
9	Positions	2
10	Open Access	1
11	Limited Access	1
12	No Access	2

ENTER THE VALUES IN THE WORKSHEET CELLS LABELED "OPEN ACCESS", "LIMITED ACCESS" AND "NO ACCESS". THE EXAMPLES SHOWN ARE: 1, 1 AND 2.

---

[6] A home with four windows may have four "fighting" positions, but the home is a single Position for this entry.

6. Assets

The military uses the phrase "Order of Battle", which I have always thought was a bit confusing. One might think they were talking about the sequential steps that were to take place during a battle, or what orders would be issued during the fight.

In reality, the term "Order of Battle" refers to the list of assets and capabilities available for the mission. How many troops, tanks, and other assets the commanders have at their disposal.

For our planning purposes, I will use the term Assets.

Your Asset Inventory is a constantly changing list. I have a teenage son who has equal capabilities and skills to my own. He is as asset, but will eventually leave the house. When he does, my asset inventory will change.

The Assets available to you after an event may not all be your own. I have a neighbor who has a swimming pool. He plans to "bug out", so I have an asset of several thousand gallons of water available if he executes his plan.

For the purposes of our calculations, the following is a list of assets we should note at this time.

6.1 Number of Defenders

The Number of Defenders is the actual count of the people who will be defending your location. This should be the count of anyone who can participate in the defense, but should <u>NOT</u> include dependents. Be realistic here – don't confuse your heart, ego or mindset with actual experience and skills. Even if no one in your group has ANY experience or skills, you can easily fix that. For right now, you need an accurate inventory of skills and capabilities.

On our worksheet, you do not enter a value for Number of Defenders as it will be calculated for you as you fill in the other counts. If you are filling in the form, the Number of Defenders should equal the individual counts in each category.

> **No Firearms Experience** – Count the number in your group who has never shot a firearm. Anyone who is frightened of or uncomfortable holding a weapon should be included here.

> **Basic Pistol Experience** – Include any people who have fired a pistol before, and are comfortable with at least holding it. They know how to aim a pistol.

> **Basic Rifle Experience** – Include the people who have shot a rifle, shotgun or other long gun before. They are comfortable holding it and could load, aim and fire a weapon once they are familiar with it.

Advanced Firearms Experience – Anyone who has formal training, avid shooters, casual hunters or others who could hit man-sized targets between 0 – 200 yards the majority of the time. Competition shooters would fall into this category as well.

Long Range Marksman – Count of everyone who can regularly hit targets at 600 meters or beyond.

Combat Vet – Military veterans, Law Enforcement Officers and others who have been shot at and had to perform.

Trained Sniper – A count of all Military Snipers or Special Forces trained people in your group. The skills these individuals are taught probably provide them the best chances of surviving in a hostile post-event environment.

I cannot stress enough that you must be conservative as you rate the members of your group. Keep in mind that the utilization of these skills will likely be after a very traumatic series of events and everyone's mental state will be affected. Try to project your thinking to that situation and then rate your group.

15	Group Factors	
16	**Number of Defenders**	4
17	No Firearms Experience	1
18	Basic Pistol Experience	0
19	Basic Rifle Experience	1
20	Advanced Firearms Experience	1
21	Long Range Marksman	1
22	Combat Vet	0
23	Trained Sniper	0

FOR EACH MEMBER OF YOUR GROUP, ENTER THEIR FIREARMS SKILL LEVEL. THE COUNT OF NUMBER OF DEFENDERS WILL CALCULATE AUTOMATICALLY AND SHOULD EQUAL THE TOTAL NUMBER IN YOUR GROUP.

6.1.1 Group Condition

The physical Condition of Group is a factor that is really a judgment call. For each defender, count them once on our worksheet in one of the following categories:

- **Restricted Mobility** – infants, toddlers, elderly, handicapped and any others who require help to move.
- **Mobile** – average mobility; can walk reasonable distances without help, can spend the day shopping or walk through the park without rest.
- **Physically Fit** – active person - tennis, golf, basketball, jogs, etc.
- **Athletic** – can run 3 miles or more or carry large amounts of weight great distances.

24	Condition of Group	
25	Restricted Mobility	0
26	Mobile	2
27	Physically Fit	1
28	Athletic	1

FOR EACH MEMBER OF YOUR GROUP, ENTER THEIR CONDITION IN THE CELLS 25 -28.

6.1.2 Dependents

The Number of Dependents should include a count of children or the elderly who cannot be counted on to assist. On our worksheet, this is the total number of people who are "dependent" on others for day-to-day activities. Non-fighters who can still help should **NOT** be counted here.

24	Condition of Group	
25	Restricted Mobility	0
26	Mobile	2
27	Physically Fit	1
28	Athletic	1
29	**Number of Dependents**	
30	**Special Skills**	
31	Basic Medical (First Aid)	1
32	Medical (RN, EMT)	1
33	Doctor	
34	Hunter	1
35	Engineer	
36	Electronics	
37	Machinst, Welder, Handyman	

ENTER THE NUMBER OF DEPENDENTS IN THE WORKSHEET CELL **29**.

6.1.3 Special Skills

This category is for anyone who has certain skills that may be critical in our defensive plan. Medical, engineering, electronics and machining come to mind. *No offense is intended for those with numerous other skills that will be critical in a post-event world. The value of someone who understands canning or can grow food will be invaluable, but this book is about defense, so we only use defense-related skills for our worksheets and formulas.* For each person that possesses a list skill, add one to the count. If someone has multiple skills, add one for each skill they possess.

- **Basic Medical** (First Aid) – a count of anyone who can perform basic first aid. *Putting Band Aids on minor cuts does not count.*
- **Medical** (RN, EMT) – advanced medical skills.
- **Doctor** – very advanced medical skills.
- **Hunter** – an accomplished hunter or woodsman, someone who can track, skin, clean and process game.
- **Engineer** – virtually any type of engineer counts here.
- **Electronics** – can repair and configure basic household electronics, such as radios, motion detectors, alarms and other items.
- **Machinist, Welder or Handyman** – basic knowledge and capabilities with either/both. Most farmers I know would fit into this category as they repair their own equipment and often machine basic parts. Someone who is considered a "handyman" would also count here as well as mechanical skills.

24	Condition of Group	
25	Restricted Mobility	0
26	Mobile	2
27	Physically Fit	1
28	Athletic	1
29	Number of Dependents	
30	Special Skills	
31	Basic Medical (First Aid)	1
32	Medical (RN, EMT)	1
33	Doctor	
34	Hunter	1
35	Engineer	
36	Electronics	
37	Machinst, Welder, Handyman	

ENTER A COUNT FOR EACH GROUP MEMBER THAT HAS SPECIAL SKILLS IN THE WORKSHEET CELLS 31-37.

6.1.4 Mindset

Mindset is probably the most important factor on this list. If you have studied any survival guides or other preparation materials, you have heard this before. Without the proper mindset, all of the firearms, training and supplies in the world will not keep you alive. Personally, the Mindset of my group is my largest single concern. A good plan will improve everyone's Mindset. Good materials, equipment and preparation will also help. When it comes to a gunfight, the Mindset is more critical than at any other time. When I talk to people about their preparations, I encounter some very common tendencies with their thinking.

They, for example, are completely unprepared for total violence. Unless they have seen combat up close and personal, they are not ready for the speed and power of the force that may confront them.

The following conversation is typical:

Prepper: "I am ready for anybody trying to take our supplies. I have a shotgun and I will use it."

Me: "How many shells does it hold?"

Prepper: "Five – I took the plug out. If they knock on my door, they are going to have a problem."

Me: "What makes you think they would knock on your door? If I am desperate, not concerned about the law or ever being punished, why would I even bother to knock on your door?"

Prepper: "Well, how else are you going to get in? I have good quality dead bolts on the doors and this is a brick house. The windows would be boarded up if it got that bad."

Me: "I would just blow your door off the hinges. I would **not** knock. We would hit your front and back doors at the same time. I would put a 12 gauge slug on each of the three hinges in less than 2 seconds and then kick the door off of the hinges. We will have people POURING in your house within 3 seconds of when you hear the first noise."

Now if you think I am being a little harsh on our fictional prepper, you are wrong. I am simply being realistic. The internet is full of videos of U.S. Marines doing house to house searches in Iraq. They were operating under rules of engagement to protect the occupants. Watch any of these videos while thinking – what if their intent was to kill the people inside the house? What if they just went in guns blazing? Would the occupants have any chance? The answer to that is most likely NO, ZERO CHANCE.

It is very difficult to develop this mindset without experience, and no one wants that type of experience. What you can do is develop a defensive plan that eliminates most of the options available to any attacker. In the above example, if the doors were reinforced, it would take longer to gain entry. They would be making all kinds of ruckus and racket in the attempt. A dog barking as they approached would provide even more warning. Military and LE professionals refer to a doorway as a "fatal funnel." What if you were up and ready, spraying lead at the doorways as the bad guys tried to enter? They can only get through one at a time – and thus the fatal funnel. The attack might fail.

I have also had this conversation more times than I can count:

Me: "It has all gone to hell. It's really bad. You are holed up in your BOL (Bug Out Location) and you see a skinny, dirty young girl with a filthy baby and toddler walking up your sidewalk. They bang on the door. What do you do?"

Prepper: "I don't open the door – I yell through and ask her what she wants".

Me: "She pleads with you that she is hungry and thirsty. She just wants some water and will leave."

Prepper: "I tell her to back away from the door and I will set her out some water. When she is well away, I open the door and set some water on the porch, maybe some food if we have plenty."

Me: "Bang! You are dead and so is everyone in your home. I was hiding two football fields away behind a tree with a rifle. She was bait. You are lying on your front porch bleeding out with the door unsecured behind you."

Prepper: "That's not fair! What am I supposed to do? Turn away someone who really might be desperate?"

Me: "Your first mistake was for your house to even look like someone might be home. Why did she choose your house? Your second mistake was to even acknowledge someone was home. While you were smart not to open the door, why did you even answer her at all? Even if she was what she appeared, if you gave her food and water, she might be back every day, over and over. Do you really think that if she was what she appeared to be, she wouldn't tell others where she got that bottle of water?"

Prepper: "So you would not have even acknowledged her pounding on the door? Just turned her away?"

Me: "If she was pounding on my door, I would be checking the other sides of the house to make sure her friends were not sneaking up on us. "

Prepper: "I can't think or live like that. That is not how I was raised."

Me: "You had better start thinking about that. No one wants to be faced with those types of decisions, but if you are going to protect your family, you need to understand the dark side. Not join it, but understand it and be prepared to deal with it."

Like so many of our other factors, there is no precise method for determining what everyone's Mindset will be in a post-event world. It is probably logical to assume that it will change several times as well. You need to know the people in your group. How do they react to an emergency? How do they handle stress? Who will get aggressive and who will turn into a puddle when threatened?

For each member of your group, count them (as well as yourself) into one of the following categories:

Timid or Unknown – children or teenagers would be examples here. Anyone you would suspect to react poorly to stress, emergencies or other situations when threatened.

Average – the typical person will surprise you in an emergency. They can normally at least take care of themselves or react rather than freeze.

Aggressive – this should be people who are veterans, played contact sports or excel at martial arts. Anyone who believes the best defense is a strong offense should be counted here.

Has your back – count the few, if any, people you KNOW you would want at your back **in a fight.** This is a rare type of relationship to have.

Initially, people make the mistake of categorizing Mindset the same as fighting skills. This is not what this category is meant to define. My wife, for example, is the typical southern lady with charm, kindness and grace. She knows how to shoot a pistol, and does so now and then, but really just to spend time with me. To meet her, you would probably put her in the *Average Mindset* category. You would be wrong. She will turn into a hellcat in *one* second if someone threatens her children. She once cut a snake IN HALF with a frying pan, and it was not even near the kids. She is a nurse with ER experience, so she has a cool head in an emergency – I KNOW SHE **HAS MY BACK** in a fight.

38	Mindset	
39	Timid or Unknown	1
40	Average	2
41	Aggressive	
42	Has your back	1
43	**Group Rating**	13.00

FOR EACH MEMBER OF YOUR GROUP, RATE THEIR MINDSET IN CELLS 39-42.

6.1.5 Asset Examples

I have given you several items that will require considerable thought on your part. In order to make sure there is clear communication, let's take some examples of fictitious people and fill in our worksheet.

Your grandfather is 75. He has hunted all his life and is still a crack shot. He fought in Korea, but saw limited combat. He gets around well, but his hearing is not so good. He could not run, nor carry a heavy load, but put a rifle in his hand and he will pull the trigger. He can walk long distances. He is a stoic, tough old bird and still hard as nails.

He gets counted in the following categories:

- o Basic Rifle Experience
- o Mobile
- o Hunter
- o Average (mindset)

Your cousin does not like guns at all. Last year at the family reunion, a kid fell from a tree and broke an arm. She ran around saying "Oh my God!" over and over again. Count her as:

- o No Firearms Experience
- o Mobile
- o Timid or Unknown

Your brother-in-law is a competitive shooter. He is a successful business man and great father. He is never rattled, nor is he hyper-aggressive. He would be counted in the following categories:

- o Advanced Firearms Experience
- o Physically Fit
- o Aggressive

6.2 The Initial Evaluation

By now, you should have entered all of the values into the worksheet or form. It will calculate or you can manually calculate, two important values:

1. The Location Rating is the amount of Defensive Capabilities your location, as defined to the worksheet, requires. The higher the number, the more capabilities you need.

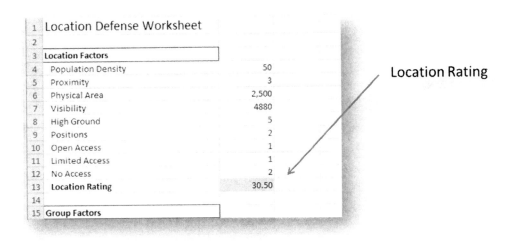

Figure 10 - Example of a Location Rating

2. The Group Rating represents the skills your group currently possesses, as related to implementing your defensive plan. The higher the number, the more capabilities, or skills, your group has.

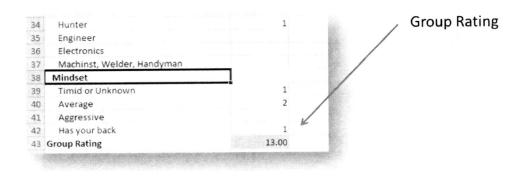

Figure 11 - Example of a Group Rating

For almost every initial evaluation performed on a new plan, the location requires more capabilities than what your group can deliver. This is normal and should not concern you. Very few domestic locations were designed to be the Alamo. When it comes to homes, our lifestyles and taste typically conflict with good defensive features. The same can be said of our group's skills. I want my kids to study, play sports and enjoy their childhood – not learn how to fight off roving gangs of food pirates.

This is the primary reason to adhere to the methodology as described in Chapter 3, specifically the dual purpose of any actions or purchases. I like to shoot and always have. I would target practice, compete and enjoy firearms even if I lived in the most secure society imaginable. For me, shooting is FUN! So it serves a dual purpose for me to max out my weapons skills as my expense and time deliver a recreational value at the same time increasing my defensive capabilities.

Many of the concepts in this book have to do with landscaping. You may be an avid gardener or have a property that could use a little touch up. A dual purpose would be served by taking into account your defensive plan before you invest in the landscaping. You have fun, improve the value of your property and sleep better at night.

6.3 Evaluation Guidelines

While no simple formula can determine the exact strength and weaknesses of every situation, there are some high level guidelines that you can use as you begin to formulate your plan.

 **If your Group Rating is less than 25, then you should consider a passive defensive strategy first.**

If your Location Rating is greater than 40, you should consider an alternative location, or Bug Out.

The remainder of this book provides solutions, ideas and concepts on how to both **LOWER** the requirements for your location as well as **RAISE** the skills and capabilities of your Group.

As you read the book, use the worksheet as a model to project the impact of your idea or plan. If you see an idea in the section on Visibility that you believe is easy to do, plug in the value in the worksheet and see how it computes the results.

As you begin to implement various parts of your preparations, pull up the worksheet or form and adjust the values to see how you are progressing.

There are also "bonus points" in the Defensive Preparations section of the worksheet. These values stress the importance of prepared fighting positions and over watch. The Defensive Rating is a guideline with any value less than 15 considered poor, 16-30 good and 30+ being a strong defensive position.

Good Luck!

6.4 The Passive Defense

As we have stated before, humans are going to be the problem. Unless you are greatly concerned about alien invasions, people are going to be what we have to defend against.

Job one of our passive defense is going to be invisibility, or stealth. No one is going to loot what they can't see or don't realize is there.

Snipers train for extended periods on not only how to shoot, but how to hide, or be invisible. They move long distances at extremely slow speeds in order to avoid detection. They study camouflage in depth. They have a trained eye on their surroundings so they know how to blend in. They use a passive profile and only go active when absolutely necessary. In most situations, discovery for them equals death.

In the preceding sections, we filled out some information about our location in order to determine how hard we will have to work to make our location invisible. The higher your ranking, the more work we are going to have to do.

6.4.1 The Facade

What if you could make your location hide in plain sight?

I once visited the filming location of an old Western TV series. All of the buildings were a façade at best and many were simply shells. That is where the idea came to me.....what if I could make my bug out location look like something completely different than what it was?

What if we could make our location look like it had been burned out?

This is really easy to do. You will need the following items:

1. Two cans of spray paint (black and grey)
2. Some old wall insulation or some from your attic
3. Scrap lumber
4. A few cardboard boxes or sheets of poster board
5. A place where you can burn a few of the items

If you ever study a building that has experienced a fire, there are some common signs anyone driving or walking by would recognize immediately. Simple things to "fake", like on a movie set would be soot or smoke that rose from the windows or insulation and burnt scraps of wood lying here or there. You can really get creative with this if you want to. Study the pictures below and I believe you will see how easy it is to make your location look like a burnt out building where there could not possibly be anything of value to raid.

Figure 12 - Example One of a Burned Out Home

If you study the picture above, you can see the smoke stains above the windows. These can be recreated with our spray paint. If the world has degraded to the point where we are implementing our plan, then spray painting the outside of our home or location is not going to be a big deal. Spray alternating colors of black and dark brown above your windows to create the smoke and fire effect. Spraying water on the wet paint helps the effect as well.

You will also note on this example, the attic area is black and burnt looking. Again, this effect is easy to create with our spray paint.

On the ground, you will see burnt insulation and wood lying around. Take our scrap lumber and spare insulation and burn them. Store them in a plastic bag and when the time comes, simply spread them around so it looks like a real fire occurred.

For a final touch, you can string up the yellow – DANGER DO NOT CROSS tape.

The example below would be easy to fake as well.

Figure 13 - Example Two of a Burned Out Home

The siding on this home is warped, and you could create the same effect with Styrofoam and paint, then, simply glue it onto the side of your house.

Our cardboard boxes are to create window treatments. If you look at the pictures above, you will notice the windows are all very dark, showing the burned out interior. You don't have to be a great artist to recreate this effect using some cardboard and paint. When the time comes, just attach the cardboard over the inside of your windows.

One of the biggest problems you may encounter in your preparations is wood burning stoves or fireplaces. Burning wood can be detected miles away. It is a sure sign of human activity for any roving bands of hostiles. Like an old TV cereal commercial said, "Just follow your nose...it always knows."

If we are faking a burnt out home, wood smoke odors would fit. If you have ever driven by a building that has burned, it smells like burnt wood for weeks.

In summary, any type of "home camouflage" or façade could be effective. I like the burned out building because some people, if looking for shelter, would be MORE LIKELY to approach an abandoned home. Few would bother looking at a fire damaged place to use as a temporary camp.

6.4.2 Large Scale Camouflage

If you have never seen 3D sidewalk art, you should do a web search on the topic and look at the pictures. They never cease to amaze me. 3D sidewalk art grew out of another form of illusion, movie set backdrops and backgrounds. Basically, it is just a painting, but from the right angle and distance, it looks REAL.

Figure 14 - Artist Drawing 3D Sidewalk Art

There is no hole, ice or snow on the ground. You can see from where the artist is standing, it is just a flat sidewalk. There are pictures of pot holes drawn on New York City sidewalks, with simple chalk, and business men are stepping around them thinking they are real.

For our purposes, drawing a hole in a sidewalk is really not useful, but the general concept can apply to disguise or block an area from view. Keep in mind, our illusion does not have to pass close-up inspection. Let's take an example of a detached garage with a walkway to the main house. There is a clean view from the street into the backyard that we need to use post-event. We do not want anyone being able to see us back there. We have several options open to us to create our illusion:

- Movable, large potted plants
- A tarp painted to match the siding on the home
- Tall scrubs
- A non-used vehicle parked at the right angle

Military snipers and many hunters use an article of clothing called a "ghillie suit." It is basically clothing with the capability to weave leaves, plants and other local colors into the suit. They are extremely effective camouflage.

Figure 15 - (Left) A Ghillie Suit. (Right) Hunter Showing the Effects of a Ghillie Suit.

The military uses very large scale camouflage netting to hide tents, bases and bunkers. If you live in a wooded area, these can be purchased or made that allow local foliage to be woven into them and are like a giant ghillie suit for a location. The military uses these devices primarily to hide from the air, but when properly applied, they can be very effective from ground level as well.

Remember, we are trying to reduce our Visibility Factor. The less visible we are, from the least number of directions, the better our security is.

A few things to remember about this type of camouflage:

- If you live where the seasons change or foliage changes colors, you need to take this into consideration. Your spring foliage green camo will stand out like a sore thumb if the ground is covered in snow.
- Your camo is going to be outside in the elements. Wind and rain can play havoc with your disguise.

Figure 16 - Can you see the tank?

Figure 17 - Visible Tank After Camouflage Net is Removed

Camouflage netting can be very effective at reducing visibility if properly applied. Like a big ghillie suit for our location, it can block a significant angle of visibility. Netting does not have to be foliage based. In a desert environment, you could paint strips of cloth to match the color of local rocks and weave them into the net. If you have trees, or other supporting structures, you can use ropes to raise or lower the nets.

The key to using netting is its location. You can't just throw a big net over your house and expect it to be effective. What you can do is string it up at the edge of a wooded area to block an angle, perhaps from a road or field. Filling in a thinner area of woods is another good application as would be blocking a utility access cut in a forest.

If your location is high on the side of a hill, you could string netting to block the view from below. Be creative – think! Walk around your BOL and find out from which areas you can see your location. Your mind if your absolute best defense.

6.4.3 Examples - Reducing Visibility

6.4.3.1   Example – The Farm

Our location is a rural farm house. It has a barn and other outbuildings and the general layout looks like the drawing below:

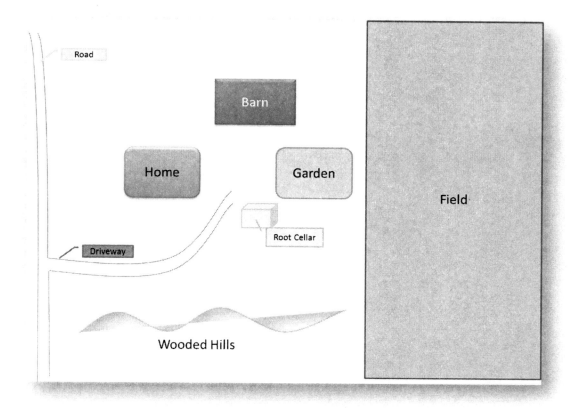

Figure 18 - Overview of a Typical Farm

First, we must outline our area of operations or activity. This is the area we are going to be using to gather food from the garden, bury our trash, cut firewood, use the well and let the kids play. We have to identify a set of boundaries or our perimeter.

This planning is a compromise in that you want to use as much area as possible, yet the more area you have the harder it is to hide and defend.

A good rule of thumb is to determine what you use on a daily basis now. If the kids have a swing set that is in the side yard, you should think about reserving that amount of space in the back yard and moving the swing set.

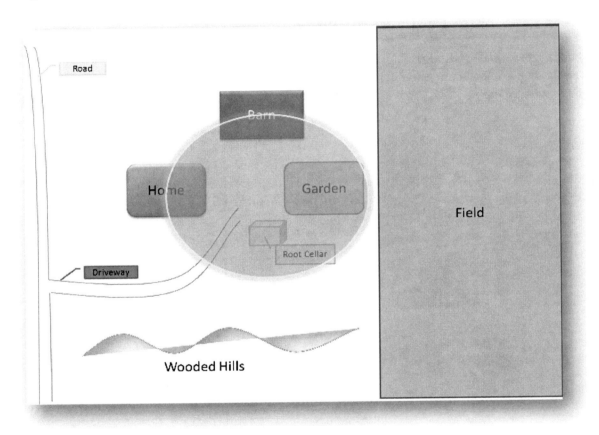

Figure 19 - Overview with Location Area (area used on a regular basis)

Another defining factor is being able to access multiple structures. In the example above, we have a barn. Like most barns, it probably is well built and perhaps even has a hay loft. Our barn gives us a second position from which to fight. The factor we filled out named "Number of Positions" above is what we are pointing out here. This may require you to install another 20 feet of privacy fence, but to have a second position is well worth it.

We need to have daily access to the garden, root cellar and barn. So we can outline that Location Area on our overview. This is the area that we have to defend. This is the area that we have to set up passive capabilities for. This is the area we are going to hide in plain sight.

Our next step is to apply the Visibility Factor we calculated above. For our example here, we have three directions from which our area is visible.

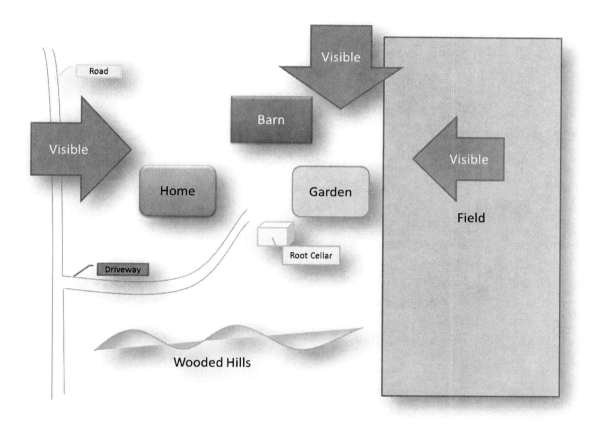

Figure 20 - Arrows indicate the three directions from which the Location Area is visible.

As you can see from Figure 20, we have three directions that have clear visibility. In order to have an active area and a passive defense, we need to block these three areas from view.

If you look at Figure 21, you can see a diagram of how we can reduce our Visibility Factor.

Our farm has large, round bales of hay, normally randomly spread around the field in back. Our first method will be to use those hay bales as a fence and line them up to block the view from the field (1). Our farm also has tractors and other large mobile equipment, so we will park those between the home and the barn (2). We may have to eventually use them, but their regular parking spot will be there.

We have to block the area between the barn and the field (3). We will do this by nailing plywood to the existing fence and making it look like a cattle run. This will raise the height to 8 feet and act like a privacy fence. The area between the home and the drive is also exposed, and we will park our normal vehicles there to block the view (4).

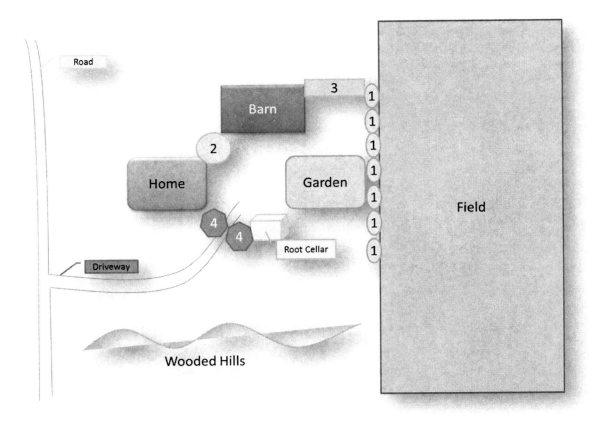

Figure 21 - Numbered objects indicate where to block visibility for the Location Area.

We have now blocked visibility from every practical angle. We also have provided reasonable cover to move from the house to the barn in the event we need two separate fighting positions. We have used natural barriers that at casual glance would be common on any farm in the area. It does not look like a heavily defended compound, but it will be when we are finished.

6.4.3.2 *Example II – The Suburban Neighborhood*
This next example is probably the most common method of housing in the United States. It is the typical suburban neighborhood that surrounds every medium to large U.S. city. While the size of the "lots" will vary with the affluence of the community, the layout is always very similar.

As you can see by the diagram below (*Figure 22*), we have rows of houses with the back yards separated by privacy fences. Our task to reduce visibility is much easier than the farm house, because the other houses and fencing blocks anyone from clearly seeing into our back yard.

If we use our Hollywood façade methods as described earlier to make our home look burned out, abandoned or already looted, then we should be able to avoid detection. We are, after all, in a target rich environment for potential looters or attackers.

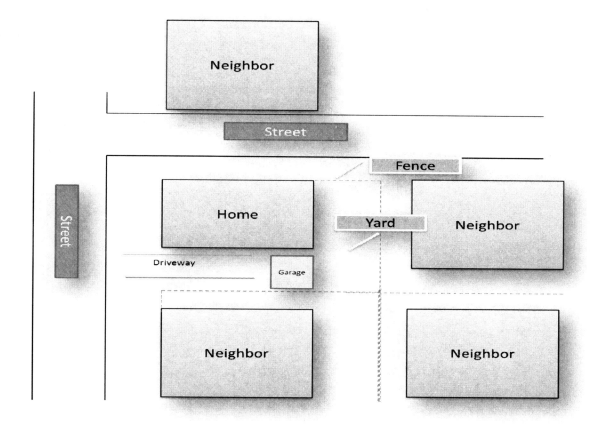

Figure 22 - Typical Neighborhood with Fenced in Yard (non-visible location area)

Our area is very limited in resources and options, but it is not the purpose of this book to cover food, water and other supplies. I have to assume you have worked all of that out.

6.4.3.3   Example III – The Rural Home

This example is the simple rural home, without the farm or the typical suburban privacy fences. The overview of this layout is shown in the Figure 23.

This is a very difficult example to reduce visibility from all directions. Because it is a rural area, we should consider the expense of blocking visibility versus a more extensive early warning system. Without ruining the property's views and openness, there is very little we can do. Since it is rural, it would take someone out "hunting" to view the property or location area and a remote location reduces the chances of that.

While it is probably a good idea to implement a façade, such as the fake fire, any observation beyond the casual glance will determine that the location is occupied.

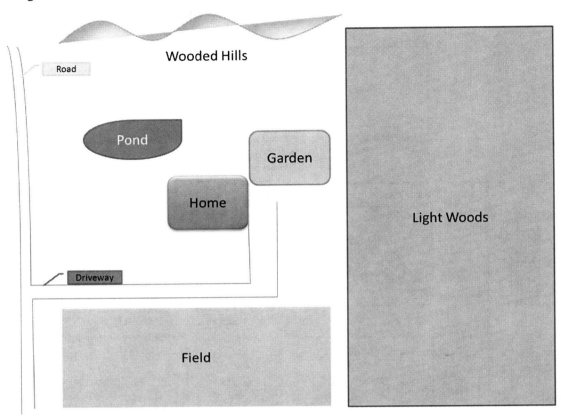

Figure 23 - Overview of a Typical Country Home

Given your budget, capabilities and the extent to which you want to create a passive defense, there are a few options open for this layout (see Figure 24). First of all, there is landscaping such as tall, fast growing shrubs. They can provide a decent reduction in visibility without ruining the property (1). We can also use ghillie nets along the woods line (2), but you will have to be careful with the change of seasons. An 8-10 foot high rope and pulley system would allow for you to quickly raise and lower the nets in order to provide a visibility barrier.

In this example, the pond may be your primary source of water for the long term. The daily walk to the pond to fill buckets would completely expose the person making the trip. The pond itself may be attractive to someone passing by to fill up a canteen. Not a good situation. Without ruining the view of the pond from the house, there is little that can be done pre-event. After the event, if you believe the need is serious enough, a quickly installed privacy fence (3) would be a good option. Planting some fast growing trees between the road and the pond (4) might also be a consideration.

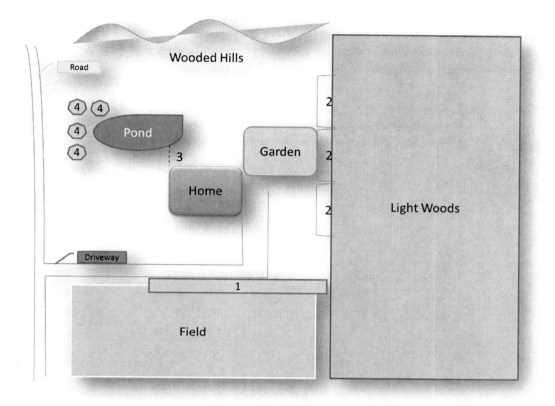

Figure 24 - Rural Home with Numbered Options to Reduce Visibility

As you can see by our diagrams and examples, where you place gardens, out buildings and even park your vehicles can make a significant difference in how exposed your Location Area is.

Of course, there are many other configurations of houses, but the examples we have considered here should help you design your specific plan for your specific location.

6.4.4 Other Options

Blocking the visibility for your Location Area can be accomplished with any mobile unit large enough to block a significant amount of view. Some examples would be:

> Semi-truck trailers
> RV's
> Camping trailers
> Hay or grain wagons
> School buses

Any of these items could be used in lieu of privacy fences, shrubs or ghillie nets. While the average American household probably does not include the above list of items, we are planning for life altering-events and the breakdown of society. Could you obtain them or scavenge a few of these in order to increase the effectiveness of your passive defenses?

You should take any potential reductions in your Visibility Factor and apply them to your Worksheet. This can have a positive impact on your location and plans.

6.5 The Active Defense

Many of the concepts outlined for a passive defense can work to your advantage in an active defense as well. Since we are not trying to "hide", but project strength and danger to anyone within range, we can use our Hollywood façade techniques to make our "defensive chest stick out."

How hard would it be to manufacture a realistic looking belt-fed M2 Machine Gun[7] out of glue, paint and Styrofoam? How about wood?

Figure 25 - Fake (actually an Airsoft) M2 Machine Gun

While a complete façade might get you in trouble if some strong-willed, weak-minded fool came along and decided to test you, those people will probably fall prey to the Darwin principle early after the event.

Think of all of the dangerous looking things you could create with just basic skills. Remember – they don't have to pass inspection up close.

Another way that we can camouflage our true capabilities is to have everyone who is outside look like a soldier. Army Surplus stores sell complete "wardrobes" and a lot of the clothing is of high quality and very low cost. Grab some BDUs (Battle Dress Uniforms), a few load vests or plate carriers, and you are off to a great start. Think of the Halloween costumes you could create!

Anyone scouting your location could think they were looking at a rogue band of deserters - or worse. This could cause them to move on to an easier target.

---

[7] The web is full of examples of people making "fake" weapons. Some of the videos give excellent instructions and are very creative.

Signage can be another strong deterrent to the wandering masses. Here are a few examples:

WARNING There is a marksman watching you right now. **GO AWAY WHILE YOU STILL CAN!**	**DANGER** Do Not Proceed or you will be shot. **RESTRICTED ACCESS**
DANGER No spare food. No spare water. Lots of spare bullets. **LEAVE OR WE WILL GIVE YOU SOME**	**WARNING** Well armed hungry Cannibals ahead. **LEAVE OR BE EATEN**

I am sure you can come up with better signs. (*Remember, there is no rule that says you can't have a sense of humor even when talking about TEOTWAWKI.*) My point is to warn off anyone approaching your location.

6.6 Diversions and Deterrents

One should not confuse diversions and deterrents as they play two completely different roles. The Allies, in WWII, created an entirely fake army, commanded by General Patton, to "divert" German attention away from the D-Day invasion. This diversion included models, wooden tanks, equipment and even bogus radio traffic.

A deterrent is meant to keep someone from attacking you because you look, or actually are, strong. The USSR was famous for this during the cold war, making inflatable missiles and other equipment to "deter" the US via U2 and satellite photo-reconnaissance.

Regardless of an active or passive defense, setting up diversions could improve your capabilities. It would not take a large amount of additional work to use our Hollywood façade techniques in the opposite way and make a nearby home appear to be occupied or active. As you could imagine, sitting and watching a gang of looters storm an abandoned neighbor's house while your team got into position would be an advantage, perhaps even entertaining.

You could set up "noise makers" in a neighboring farm or home to confuse any attackers. In the section on Early Warning Systems (7.2) we show you how to make an "alarm" out of a mousetrap and a shotgun shell. What if you could place a few of these in the woods, or abandoned home across the field and set them off if you were being approached?

One of my favorite "training" tools is a kid's toy remote control vehicle. You can pick up rather robust ones for less than $100 and the range of the radio transmitter can be several hundred yards. We use coat hangers and attach targets to them so as to practice shooting at a "moving" bad guy. *Don't shoot the toy – they are not bullet proof!*

So if you were to make a few "noise makers", set up tripwires in the barn and run over them with the remote control toy it would create an interesting diversion. The "skinnies" may just turn and run. Battery management might be an issue, so you could also "string" tripwires to your location if the diversion site is close enough.

Making your location appear burned out or abandoned while a close-by structure appears to be occupied requires some thought. For a remote location like a ranch, the effectiveness of this might be limited depending on the distance between the two homes. It may be worthwhile to consider letting a flashlight burn through the night at a neighboring ranch with tripwires and noise makers. You should consider this carefully. If I was the leader of a nomadic band of looters, and I eventually realized I had been duped, I would KNOW someone had gone to the trouble for a reason. If I am a smart guy, I would also understand that they were now ready for me, but that is giving a protein starved mind a lot of credit. I may also be so mad that the urge for revenge takes over common sense. Since you can't predict or control what your opponent may think or do, you should choose your diversion carefully.

Most diversions only buy you time, or eliminate the threat of being surprised. Time, however, can be critical

The concept of being able to "hit" your attackers (see Spoiling Attacks in section 6.15) while their attention is focused on your diversion may be attractive as well. The wisdom of this approach depends on the capabilities of you and your group. Unless the diversion is VERY close by, it would mean you have to move away from your pre-stocked, known positions and move as an offensive force. This brings an entirely new set of skills into play and requires a completely different plan. The fact that you may be dividing your forces with a known enemy close by should be carefully considered.

6.7 Light Discipline

One of the most critical things you can do to hide your location is light discipline. If I am a bad guy, looking for places to go raid, I am going to find a high spot to climb to and look for lights. Light means humans, and that means food, water or other items I need. I could use a tree, radio tower, building roof or any other structure that allows me to gain height and thus visibility of my local area.

If the electrical grid is down, street lights don't work and any light source, even a candle or small flashlight can be seen for miles. You might as well light up a big neon arrow pointing at your location and flashing "WE ARE HERE."

You will need lights, even if just small candles, at your location. It is critical that you block all windows, door cracks or other areas where light can "leak" out. If you must go outside with a flashlight, be extra, extra careful to keep it pointed down. Using a red or green light reduces its visibility at long distances.

When you are considering how to cover your windows, you should perform a few test runs to make sure shadows don't bleed through. Some other items to consider:

- You will need light during the day. If you cover ALL of your windows, the cover should be easily removable on at least some of them.
- You will need fresh air. It is probably safe to assume that you live in an area where at least some months become hot. Another reasonable expectation is that you will not have electricity, thus will need to open windows for cooling. If you live in southern regions, keeping cool should be a primary concern.

6.8 Noise Discipline

Run Silent – Run Deep

One of my biggest concerns about our location and passive defense is the generator and the noise it makes. Noise discipline is more difficult than light, water, food or movement discipline.

> *After Hurricane Rita, my neighborhood was without power for 14 days. Most of the city was down for at least 3 days. Our area is normally very quiet but I was shocked that first morning by how quiet it was outside. It was like being in the middle of a desert, not next to a city of four million people.*

> *It took a few hours for all of us to get our generators out, hooked up and started. I could easily tell when my neighbor got his going from the noise. It was not long before the neighborhood sounded more like an Indy Car Race than a suburban area.*

I walked our street a little later that day to check on folks I had not seen yet and make sure no one needed help with any big limbs. People were mostly outside surveying damages and it was amazing how difficult it was to hold a normal conversation, out in the street, due to all of the generators running.

A running generator, the sounds of children playing in the back yard (they are going to have to do SOMETHING), hammering, barking dogs, chopping wood and the noise generated by these activities is likely to attract predators. If I am "hunting", and I hear the now unusual noise of a motor running, I am going to know immediately that someone has fuel, perhaps electrical power and most likely food. The sound will lead me right to you.

The best method for noise discipline is to develop a submarine mentality of Run Silent – Run Deep. The obvious problem here is that submarines normally have warning when a foe is near, so they switch from normal operations to silent operations when that warning is received. Submarines are mobile as well, and your location probably is not. You cannot sneak away.

Most large yachts have a generator, similar to the one you use at home. On a yacht, low noise levels are critical and the generator manufactures try to equip their generators with "sound shields." While the shields are effective, you can still hear the generator running for quite a distance. These sound-shielded units cost a lot more than a normal, portable household generator and yet they could still be detected at some distance. Without a lot of expense and trouble, there is really no good way to silence a generator.

That can be said of children as well.

When Hurricane Rita hit, my kids were 12 and 9 years old. They had seen thunderstorms knock out power before, so it was no big deal for them. They knew their jobs and retrieved the candles and flashlights and pre-positioned them throughout the house for that night. We kept them busy that first day helping me pick up tree limbs, raking the yard, setting up the camping stove and other activities. The first night was sort of interesting as we played cards and board games by candle light (we only use our generator for the freezer, refrigerator and to run fans in the bedroom).

By the third day, the honeymoon was over. It was very hot and everyone was a little short tempered. The kids were bored, wanted to watch TV and began pestering me to unplug the freezer for an hour so they could watch TV. While this would have been easy to do, I was reluctant because it would be a bad habit to start and I wanted to "make them a little tougher." Besides, we had heard on the radio that the power company trucks were swarming the city and entire neighborhoods were having their power restored.

By the fifth day, we were beginning to think that our neighborhood was last on the list for grid repair. It was. This stressed the adults. The weather was very hot and I think we were all developing a short fuse. I decided letting the kids watch a DVD powered by the generator was not such a bad idea.

On the 8th day, we almost lost the food in the refrigerator because I forgot to switch the plug back from the kids watching a DVD. We were all sick and tired of each other, and the kids were now spending more and more time outside and playing with the other bored kids on the block. They were about the only thing you could hear above all of the generator noise.

*Gasoline was now available in most of the area, so it became a treat to sit in the running (**i.e. more noise**), AC equipped truck and watch a movie in there. We even cooked popcorn on the camping stove one night and all of us sat and watched a movie on the truck's little entertainment screens.*

As more time went by, the truck, due to its AC, was becoming more and more popular. The kids even wanted to sleep out there.

Given enough time and expense, you can reduce the sound created by a generator. Of course, a solar power system is silent if you decide to spend your funds there. Sound shielding materials are expensive and you would have to be handy to build a structure around your generator that still allowed access for refueling and other maintenance. I will warn you ahead of time, you will not be able to make it completely silent regardless of how much effort you put into it.

What you can do about generator noise is reduce it and hope for the best.

- Install a muffler on the motor. There are numerous internet sites where people have purchased automotive mufflers with great results.
- Build a generator shroud or tent. If you do a web search of "sound proofing technology", you will see there are numerous companies that make various materials that deaden sound. Several of these are very flexible and similar to a thick cloth or canvas. You could build a Generator Tent with simple poles and stakes.
- Build a sound shield around the unit if you won't have to move it often and have the room to store the shield and the generator. Be careful to allow for cooling.

Overall, in a passive defense, noise is going to be one of the biggest problems with hiding in plain sight. You can have your location camouflaged to the nth degree, but if the bad guys are walking close by and hear your children playing in the back yard, they will find you.

We will cover Early Warning Systems in section 7.2 and this will provide some insurance, but above all other aspects of your post-event life, the noise you generate should be one of the largest considerations for your plan.

Make sure you have a plan for the kids to keep them quiet. Older children will understand, but some sort of "quiet game" or other method should be tested on the younger ones. If I were the parent of younger children, I would have to seriously consider a bug out plan over a bug in. A lot of children can't be quiet in church, let alone on a daily basis in a stressful situation. Most of us have heard the "campfire" quiz about the mother with the crying baby while trying to hide from certain death. How does she keep the baby quiet? Would she sacrifice the baby to save everyone in the group? Would you?

A bug out plan to a more remote area (less population density, thus less chance of other people being within earshot) would be attractive to me if I had younger children.

6.9 Trash Discipline

I will include both litter and latrine discipline in this section, because the problem is similar. There are really only two solutions available for litter – bury it or burn it. Digging trash pits is a lot of work. The same can be said of latrines. While most modern toilets will function if you have water in the reserve tank, some urban sewage systems will eventually fail leaving you with a problem regarding human waste. Even in a Spartan, post event lifestyle, you will be surprised at how much trash you will generate. Burning the trash leads to smoke, odor and ash piles. Even with a wood burning stove, there is a lot of garbage that you won't want to stick in there. Burning large trash piles is not a great method when hiding in plain sight. The best method is to dig the trash pits and latrines.

I know of a few preppers who plan to tote their garbage away from their primary location and burn it. I don't like this idea, because of the security risk it imposes during the trip and the smell/smoke. Another common idea is to carry it away and just dump it, but if I am the boogie man and I find fresh trash, I am going to sit, watch and follow you back home. I might just ambush you right then and there.

An outhouse fixes the latrine problem and may be a worthwhile pre-event project if you don't have your own septic system or water supplies are limited.

If you live in a region where the ground freezes during winter months, you might want to plan ahead on digging your trash pits.

6.10 An Overgrown Mess

If you are going passive, your location should reveal ZERO indication of being occupied. That means no mowing the grass, or no tracks through any area that is visible. If I am "hunting" and I see a home with worn trails through the overgrown front yard, I know someone is probably home or at least walking through the area on a regular basis.

- If you have two cars in the driveway, and you are not using them, move one and flatten a tire on the other.
- Go scavenge a "For Sale" real estate sign and put it up in your front yard. One that says "Foreclosure" is even better.
- Take some junk out of the garage and spread it around your yard. Make your location look like it has already been looted. The looters are probably who "set it on fire", wink, wink.
- If you have large trees close to the house, find a tree limb nearby and prop it up against the side of the house like it fell there and no one was there to clean it up.
- Paint the inside of your window blinds or window treatments to make the glass look broken. If you are making window inserts to block light, make them look like plywood or boards nailed across the window.

Given the current condition of real estate, it should not be difficult to find homes in your area that are abandoned. You should take pictures and study them. What is different about homes that are clearly unoccupied?

The real objective here is to plan and equip for being able to make your location (home) look empty and worthless to anyone passing by. You should be able to do this in a reasonable amount of time.

You should also take care not to give any indication, from any direction that has visibility, that anyone is occupying the location.

- Keep children only in a non-visible area, such as the fenced in back yard
- Don't put any rain catches, trash pits or other signs of life where it can be seen from the visible directions.
- Figure out where you can hang laundry or allow clothes to dry without it being seen. Fresh clothes on a line are a SURE SIGN that someone is home, active and well fed.

6.11 Multiple Angles of Fire

Even if our defense is primarily passive, we have to be ready if discovered. One of the first determinations you must make is the number of places you can fight from. This is referred to as "multiple angles of fire", or how many directions from which you can shoot at attackers.

If all of your defenders are close together, the attacker has a small primary area to worry about, take cover from and focus their shots at. If you have two or more angles to shoot from, you double their problems for each angle. Using our farm as an example, we can diagram (*Figure 26*) three positions that would give any potential attacker serious issues to deal with.

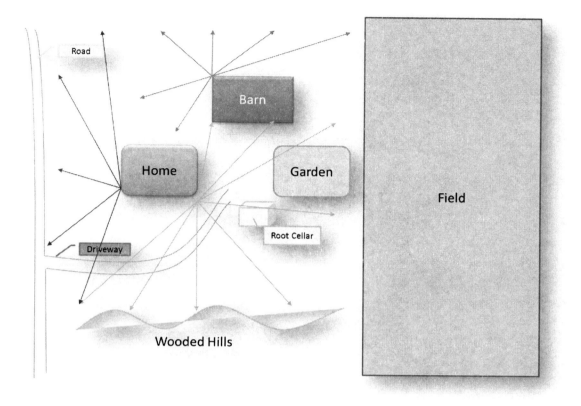

Figure 26 – Arrows Showing Fields of Fire from 3 Positions

As you can see from the arrows, just three defenders can provide almost 360 degree coverage if positioned correctly. The problem is that it is almost impossible to position defenders like this. A lot of people think like the above diagram, but it just won't work. It is important to take a minute to figure out why now, rather than later when you don't have the time to deal with it.

To begin with, you will most likely be using a window opening as your position. It just makes sense and has been a common defensive position in urban warfare for thousands of year. Unless you are going to cut firing slots in your walls, or build sandbagged machine gun nests in your yard (not real stealthy), you really have little choice in the matter.

So look around your location and count how many windows you have that are RIGHT on the corner of your home. The number is probably a big, fat **ZERO**. We just don't build homes that way. If you are lucky, you will have windows that are close to the corner of your home like the next diagram.

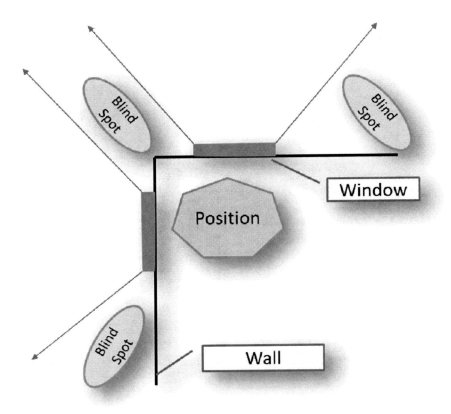

Figure 27 - Arrows Indicate Clear Fields of Fire for a Defender in Position

Even in this situation, we still have significant blind spots to deal with. If you ever watch video of real police or military teams entering a building, they know and understand these blind spots. It is just instinctive to be against the walls, especially if someone is shooting at you.

There are some basic options to deal with this problem:

1. Simple mirrors mounted to increase your angle of view and stop someone before they can enter the blind spots. You see them in stores all the time so clerks can look "around" corners.
2. Area Denial Systems – or devices that "cover" the blind spots for you. The military would use mines, barbwire or other devices to deny these blind spots.
3. Angles via Groups – having someone in the barn could cover one whole side of your home. Just don't shoot each other!
4. 90 degree optics – they actually make rifle and optic accessories that allow you to "see" around a corner without exposing yourself. Similar to a mirror, they can provide a solution.

The mirrors are simple enough to understand and could be mounted quickly and easily. You just have to hope they don't get shot out during a fight.

Area Denial Systems are a much more complex and sensitive issue for all of us. It is illegal to build or own such devices in most parts of the world. So unless you have access to military supplies (unlikely) or are an explosives expert, this all gets a little dicey to say the least. One could speculate that if we ever needed such items, concern about legality would be the least of our worries, and I somewhat agree. After all, we are preparing for actions that would be unnecessary if government was still providing security. We will cover the details of Area Denial Systems (section 6.16).

One could also speculate that if the "event" ever did occur, we could build our own mines, booby traps and devices, but I have to caution here – It is NOT as simple as it sounds. Several books have been written on how to manufacture homemade explosives and dozens of people have been hurt trying to do so. If you know there is no medical care available, are you really going to try and cook up a batch of explosives in your kitchen? Even if you did, can you store, deploy and safely disconnect such items? How are you going to test your work? Unlike a rifle, you can't go to a public range and make sure your mixture is correct.

My biggest single concern about such contraptions is deployment. For our defensive purposes, we need either a directional device that impacts a specific direction (like military claymore mines) so we don't hurt ourselves or we would need timed devices, like a hand grenade. This all becomes very technical or requires materials most of us don't have access to.

Figure 28 - U.S. Army Issued Claymore Mine

I have even read web pages that purport to show instructions on how to take common shotgun shells and make wide area anti-personal weapons out of them. These things look dangerous and I would probably end up blowing myself or a family member apart. At minimum, the dog running around the yard would be in great danger.

Like everything else in this book, this is ultimately up to you. Personally, I am going to go with diligence in setting up my positions and have a nice supply of small mirrors available.

 IF YOU DO HAVE <u>TRUE</u> MULTIPLE ANGLES OF FIRE, SUCH AS THE BARN IN FIGURE 23, YOU SHOULD INCREASE THE COUNT FOR POSITIONS ON OUR WORKSHEET. SINCE THE VALUE ASSOCIATED WITH POSITIONS HAS A SIGNIFICANT IMPACT ON OUR LOCATION RATING, YOU SHOULD BE SURE THAT IT TRULY IS A DIFFERENT ANGLE.

6.11.1   Angles via Groups

If you have like-minded neighbors, the absolute best way to achieve multiple angles is to have a pact with those neighbors. **An attack on one is an attack on all.** In a suburban neighborhood this might be relatively easy to arrange. For a remote location it becomes complex in that the nearest neighbor may be a long distance away. To expect neighbors to travel a distance to help defend your location may be asking a lot. This would depend on the relationship, the neighbor's capability and your ability to reciprocate in kind.

As an example scenario, the Jones family lives half a mile away. The Event occurs and you and Mr. Jones make a mutual defense pack – you will help each other if attacked or raided.

In a few weeks, gun shots wake you up in the middle of the night. You look towards the Jones place and can see flashes and hear more shots. It sounds like a war down there. You now have a dilemma. You gave your word, but never thought about it being at night. The concept of dressing, loading up weapons and walking right into that situation does not sound like a good idea. Should you stay at home to protect your family? What if you get shot by Mr. Jones by accident? Will the bad guys head towards your place? Will you run into them on the way there? What if the Jones family decided to bail out and is heading towards your place? The entire scenario could be maddening.

Moving at night in a hostile environment under stress is NOT easy. Leaving your location when known bandits are in the area would make the entire affair even more difficult. Making an agreement with a neighbor should be well thought out. Don't let bravado or ego get you into a situation that you are unequipped or ill prepared to deal with. It will do neither party any good.

If both parties have good size groups, a high level of skill can make a solid plan on signals, approach and action, having the cavalry show up to provide multiple angles of fire can make all the difference.

This book contains other sections that address safety in numbers, and it is correct that there is safety in angles as well. The only drawback in having a supporting location, such as your neighbor, is that you run the danger of shooting at each other during the fog of battle. If you put yourself in the role of the looter's leader, each angle you have to deal with exponentially increases your problems and risk.

Figure 29 shows a single location and the general fields of fire (arrows) from that location. If I am leading the looters, I have to worry about cover and approach from a single direction. I can converge all of my firepower on that location. I can envelop from two directions at once - if I am smart enough or have enough control to do so.

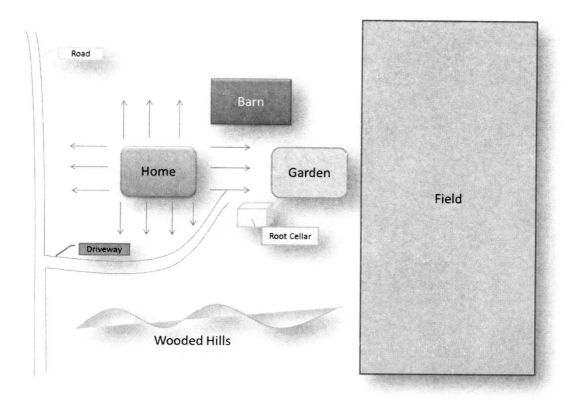

Figure 29 - Arrows Indicate Fields of Fire from a Single Angle

You as the defender have to cover 360 degrees of your location. For a small group, this is difficult at best. An enveloping attack would allow the enemy to get very close and then one of your advantages as a defender is negated.

But what if there was a plan with the Jones family? Let's say that Mr. Jones was a capable man and you both were smart enough to plan all of this out ahead of time. You both could cause our ficticious raiders a lot of problems. Here is a summary of what this plan should include:

- Approach
- Position
- Arrival Signal
- Acknowledgement Signal
- Action

- Help Signal
- End Action and Recovery

The first item the plan has to address is <u>where</u> will Mr. Jones approach our location from? We don't want to shoot him by mistake. This should be agreed upon ahead of time because at night, during the stress and fog of battle, mistaken identity is possible.

The second part of the plan must be what position Mr. Jones is going to use to fight from. This is critical in that we don't want him fixed <u>and</u> exposed. This position should be well thought out. You should be able to support him from your location as well. Multiple angles of fire are an advantage from BOTH directions.

The third item our plan has to make clear is the <u>signal</u> that will inform you that Mr. Jones has arrived. A common signal would be a flare, flashing light or prearranged radio signal. This is important for reasons beyond mistaken identity. First of all, you will want to reposition your defenders given that you now have help. Secondly, the looters may detect Mr. Jones before you do and re-focus on his position. You need to "have his back."

The fourth element of our plan needs to be an <u>acknowledgment</u> signal back to Mr. Jones that you are aware he is there. He needs to know you are aware of his presence.

In reality, any raiding party, when confronted with this situation would probably decide to high-tail it out of there. Most likely our attackers are not highly motivated to risk it all for a single farm house that is obviously well defended and is now reinforced.

However, there is no way to know how protein starved minds are going to react, so we should continue with our plan.

Once Mr. Jones is in position and acknowledged, you have several options to end the raid. Since the likelihood of either party being skilled at infantry maneuvers is low, Mr. Jones's primary action should be to lay down fire. Again, communication is critical. You, on the other hand, need to cover his flanks (sides) or "keep the enemy off of him."

There should be additional signals for if he needs help. While your options may be limited in helping Mr. Jones, the signal has merit all the same.

The final piece of the plan should be the cease fire signal. Again, blue-on-blue friendly fire is to be avoided at all costs.

A simple plan like this can be very effective. Figure 30 shows the problems just two angles of fire can create for an attacker.

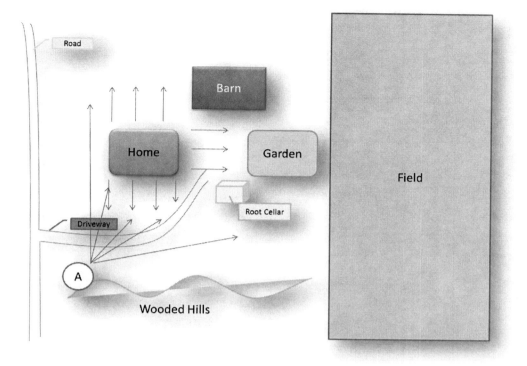

Figure 30 - Another Angle Reduces the Attacker's Options

Mr. Jones's position is marked as "A" on Figure 30. His mere presence, even if he is not the greatest shot at the skeet club, will cause serious issues for anyone attacking.

Two sides of the farmhouse have been eliminated for possible enveloping attack.

The defenders now have one less side of the home to worry about (you still have to cover Mr. Jones, so you don't gain two sides). Anyone between Mr. Jones and the home are in a cross fire and not likely to stay there long.

This 2nd angle of fire has also removed an egress route from our attackers. Every advantage you eliminate means the attack is less likely to succeed.

For suburban locations, with closer neighbors, your pact is much simpler. Since most of your neighbors are within weapons range or "right down the street", you don't need as detailed plan or signals.

Figure 31 shows a single location and the general fields of fire (arrows) from that location. If I am leading the looters, I have to worry about cover and approach from a single direction. I can converge all of my firepower on that location. I can envelop from two directions at once, if I am smart enough or have enough control to do so.

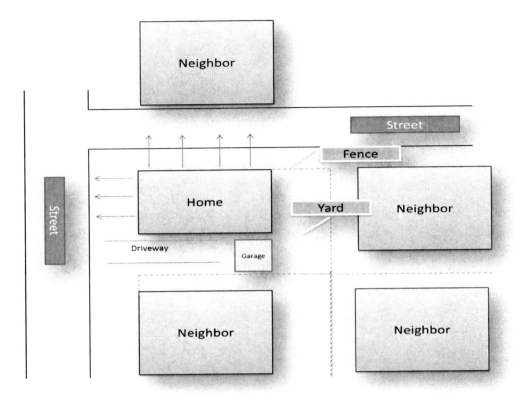

Figure 31 - Arrows Indicated Fields of Fire from a Single Home

We can cause our looting party a lot of problems if our neighbor responds to our attack. Figure 32 illustrates this by showing the neighbor's fields of fire.

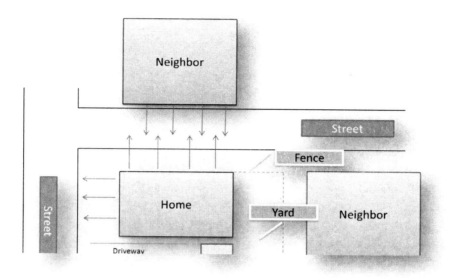

Figure 32 - Adding Another Angle Reduces an Attacker's Options

As you can see above, the looters can now only use a direct, frontal attack. The option to envelop has been removed. A direct attack, in the case from the left hand street, allows the defenders to concentrate all of their fire in a single direction. A direct attack would almost certainly fail.

In addition, this 2nd angle of fire has removed an egress route from our attackers. We keep removing advantages the attacker has. If we had a three-way pack, with a neighbor across the left hand street (not shown), we now have the attackers in a real bad situation.

This 3rd angle of fire would be similar in effect as an ambush and every soldier I have ever met fears the ambush as much as any threat they face.

ANY AGREEMENT WITH YOUR NEIGHBORS THAT ESTABLISHES OR CREATES A SECONDARY OR ADDITION ANGLE SHOULD INCREASE THE COUNT OF "POSITIONS" ON THE WORKSHEET. THE VALUE OF MULTIPLE POSITIONS IS VERY HIGH IN THE CALCULATIONS.

CAUTION SHOULD BE TAKEN WHEN COUNTING ON "NON-CORE" MEMBERS OF A GROUP IN THAT THEY MIGHT NOT BE HOME, OR MAY NOT BE ABLE TO PULL THE TRIGGER. BE CONSERVATIVE WITH ANY ASSUMPTIONS.

6.12 Fighting Positions

Of all of the preparations included in this book, I believe this is one of the most commonly misunderstood topics. First of all, I will attempt to overcome some myths propagated by years of watching Hollywood movies.

1. Walls are **NOT** bullet proof. Even brick or stone exterior walls will not stop a medium caliber round. The old movies where the hero hides beside the window frame while bullets buried themselves into the wood are absolutely not true.
2. Almost anything flammable will catch fire if you shoot it enough. I grew up next to an open air garbage dump. It was a common weekend destination to 'go shoot the rifles at the dump'. People dumped just about anything they wanted there, including construction waste, old cars, household appliances and furniture. I have caught more household items on fire by shooting at them than I can count. Vacuum cleaners, old stoves, couches…you name it, I have made it flame just by shooting it. There is no doubt that most window treatments (drapes) will burn easily.
3. You cannot shoot a large weapon in an enclosed space and expect to hear anything for hours unless you have hearing protection. If the space is close enough, you may lose an ear drum. In our plans, communication during any attack is going to be critical, so you need to be able to hear.
4. Vehicles make horrible cover. A car/truck door will not stop a bullet. The wheels and engine block provide the best cover, but even these are **NOT** 100% bullet proof.
5. People can run and shoot accurately at the same time. This is **FALSE**; with the exception of maybe a very, very few highly trained professionals. Paul Howe, the owner of CSAT (www.combatshootingandtactics.com) and one of the actual **Delta Force** members depicted in the movie and book *BLACKHAWK DOWN*, writes this about shooting on the move:

"Reference shooting on the move. It is a skill that all shooters aspire to learn and spend a great deal of time and effort trying to master. I have never had to use it in combat. When moving at a careful hurry, I stopped planted and made my shots. When the bullets were flying, I was sprinting from cover to cover, moving too fast to shoot. I did not find an in between. If I slowed down enough to make a solid hit when under fire, I was an easy target, so I elected not to."

This is important to consider because the typical attacker will not just run straight at you, but will be running from cover to cover or crawling. When selecting fighting positions, you should keep this in mind.

Regardless of the construction, layout or terrain of your location, there are common, key elements to any fighting position:

1. Observation
2. Cover
3. Stealth
4. Comfort and Maintainability
5. Accessibility

In addition, our methodology (Chapter 3) should always be considered.

Observation is important because we hope to be "watching" more than "shooting", and even if a fight does break out, you still have to see your attackers to defend yourself.

Cover, or stopping bullets, is obvious. Someone may be shooting at you.

Stealth is critical because you never know if you will be scouted. This also applies because we don't want to harm the value of our property. We will probably be doing some pre-event work and have to consider our methodology.

Comfort and Maintainability are included because we may be in our position for extended periods of time. Keeping watch may become a common task and that means staying alert. Cramps, lack of water or fatigue can distract any sentry.

Accessibility means that we should be able to get into the position quickly. I have a window in my attic that would be a great fighting position except that it takes forever to get up there and that makes it worthless. Chapter 7, The Perimeter, addresses this in more detail.

We will cover three types of positions: interior, exterior and over watch. Interior positions are those within your home or building. Exterior positions are outside of a structure. Over watch is a high ground position, interior or exterior.

Before we progress though these different types of positions, we will address some of the common elements.

It is difficult, if not impossible, to find fighting positions in the typical home that easily meet all of our elements. Since we cannot easily move windows, walls, doorways or trees, observation becomes our highest priority in the selection process. You can't fight what you can't see. All of the other factors can be addressed with a good plan, some creativity and a little work.

Everyone should understand that the critical part of a gun fight is normally executed close to the ground. Most attackers are not going to walk up to your house standing upright. They will be bent over running, crawling, or hiding behind cover. You have to take this into consideration as you begin to select your fighting positions.

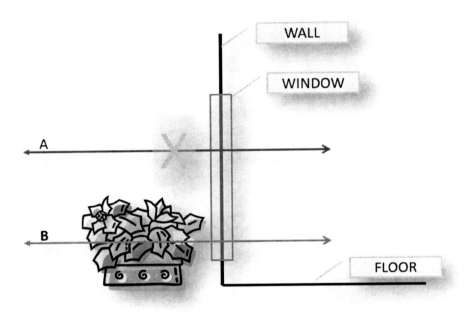

Figure 33 - Cutaway of Window

Figure 33 depicts a side view of a potential window fighting position. Most preppers will initially visualize defending this position at the level of line A. This is incorrect as line B is the level where most fighting will occur. In our drawing, we have landscaping blocking our field of fire and observation. You should look at all possible positions to ensure they allow for both.

This is important to consider when reinforcing the postion as well. The first step you should take is to determine what height your cover should be for each specific candidate. You also need to consider what physical position your body will be in so that you can comfortably shoot. For most people, it would be prone (on your belly), but window height or your physical condition may prohibit this. If you have phycial limitations, you need to determine how you can remain in a protected postion for an extended period and then build your cover around that stance. Keep in mind, you will most likely be keeping a long watch more than fighting from any postion.

While the mental picture of a favorite recliner surrounded by sand bags may be somewhat humorous, comfort will increase your dilegence and capabilities. I personally have a couple of old folding lawnchairs that are lightweight and portable. My plan includes placing these next to my fighting positions post-event. Should I have need, I can go prone behind my bullet stops quickly. A few of our windows are several feet off of the ground (over the kitchen sink), and I have no choice but to use these because of observation angles. They will require more creativity to provide good cover.

Once you determine what positions provide the best observation, then you must think about angles. Most homes are elevated above street level or yard level. For drainage, the typical yard "slopes down and away" from the home so that water can drain.

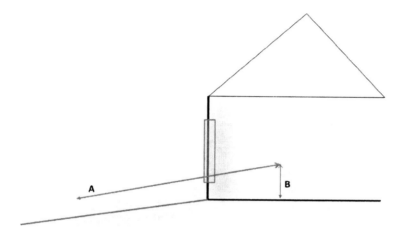

Figure 34 - Cutaway Showing Slope and Height of Position

As you can see in Figure 34, the more elevation your location has above surrounding land, the higher your bullet stop (B) needs to be. You must maintain your angle of fire (A).

The best method to compute height is to use a measuring tape to simply go try it. Pick your spot, get into a comfortable firing position and measure it.

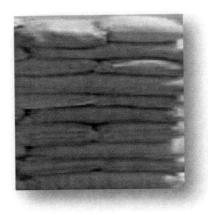

Cover is the primary purpose of creating fighting positions. Stopping high velocity lead without using our body is the goal. With a little knowledge, creativity and planning, this can be accomplished using several different methods.

As stated above, walls do not stop bullets, so we have to reinforce our fighting positions for protection.

I have read several web sites that contain plans for "ballistic plywood", "fiberglass bullet shields" and other techniques for establishing a bullet stop around your fighting position. One television show even used phone books as armor plating and it worked…somewhat. I have never tried any of these because I don't feel they are practical. If you feel confident about these methods, it may be a good solution for your location.

If you have ever heard the phrase "cheaper than dirt", it will take on a whole new meaning as you begin to develop cover (bullet stops). Good old dirt (or sand) is probably the absolute best material to consider when creating any sort of cover.

The sandbag is the simplest method to "contain" or "provide structure for" dirt.

The military uses sandbags for bullet stops or to reinforce fighting positions. Good enough for them, good enough for me. Sandbags have several advantages:

1. They are portable. You don't have to ruin the interior of your house making a bullet shield. If the event occurs, then you can mess up your wife's dining room.
2. They are repairable. It one gets ripped or torn, just apply duct tape.
3. Sand makes a great fire extinguisher.
4. Sand bags make a great rifle rest.

And the most logical reason of all:

THEY ARE DIRT CHEAP!

There is actually a recommended way to stack sand bags, but I really don't think it makes much difference.

A 5.56 NATO round (AR15), will penetrate about 10 inches of sand. A 7.62 x 51 round (.308) will penetrate about 12 inches of sand. The actual penetration depends on the type of round, distance from the target, humidity and wind. The numbers above are just averages and even if the round does go all the way through the sandbag, most of its energy will be depleted.

We don't have to use sand "bags", or even sand. Gravel (fine) or dirt will do just fine as a bullet stop and virtually any sort of "container" will work.

I have a problem window at my BOL that is perfect for observation, but is going to be a difficult to reinforce. It is in a niche that just won't work for stacking sandbags. There is a typical old wooden dresser not far away, so I plan to empty the drawers, move it in front of the window and then fill each drawer with sand and put it back in the dresser. Not perfect, but a "sandbag" nonetheless.

Obviously, having a source of sand is necessary. My BOL has a small stream nearby. I plan on backing up the pickup truck and shoveling sand into the bed for fill. If you have to dig trash pits or latrines, you have a good source of fill. A child's sandbox can work as well as landscaping top soil from non-critical areas. Most home improvement stores sell pre-bagged sand, and while this may present a storage problem, you can find a source of good fill almost anywhere.

As we proceed through our different types of fighting positions, you will find several other ideas on cover or reinforcing a position.

6.12.4   Exterior Positions

As we progress with our plan, we should include Exterior Positions. In all likelihood, we will be outside of our primary dwelling at least part of the time and may not have time to get back inside. Exterior positions normally offer more angles of fire and observation. Since we have a requirement for stealth, it is recommended that exterior positions not be obvious. You never know when someone is watching and taking notes.

There are several common items that would not look out of place in the average yard. One of my favorite examples is trash cans. Most of us have some sort of outside trash containers or cans. Mine are large, black plastic units on wheels. I could tip them on their sides and fill them as much as possible with sand bags, dirt or gravel and they would make an excellent fighting position. In a post-event world, I probably would have little use for them anyway.

Another great "nest" or fighting position could be raised flower beds. These can be rectangle shaped wooden boxes about the size of a watering trough for livestock or simple mounds of dirt bordered with railroad ties.

I am constantly looking around for a good position to fight from. Do you have a row of firewood alongside of a car port? Do you have landscaping boulders in your yard?

Another concept would be a tree house for the kids. When I was a lad, my mother (yes, my mom) built me the most outstanding tree house you ever saw. It had a trap door, rope ladder and was a great observation point for my numerous battles with savages, German infantry, and any other invaders that might dare test the firepower of my BB gun. Now that I am a bit older and can hit a target at over 900 meters, I think about that tree house and how difficult it would be to move me out of it if properly equipped and reinforced with bullet stops. This concept is covered in the next section titled "Over Watch."

Count the number of Exterior Fighting Positions you have set up and enter them into the worksheet cell labeled "Exterior Positions." Unless you are simply modeling to justify the cost, don't count them unless all of the materials are ready and the position has been improved, including the pre-positioned supplies.

6.12.5   Over Watch

One very effective fighting position is the rooftop. If you have ever seen the President of the United States in person, or watched documentaries about the Secret Service protecting him, you will notice that they take the high ground and occupy the roof tops. The reasons are two-fold; deny those areas to a potential threat and to provide "over watch" capabilities. The old adage of "take the high ground" is really true and with modern optics and some marksmanship skills. This sort of position can be extremely potent. Some basic items to consider for a roof top or elevated fighting position are:

1. Access to the position should be binary, in other words, once the position is occupied you can deny it to anyone else. An example here would be a rope ladder that can be pulled up so no one can have access to you.
2. The position should NOT silhouette the defender.
3. The position should be sheltered and camouflaged as much as possible. You may be up there for a while and hot sun or cold wind can make it unmanageable or ineffective.
4. If the position is not well concealed it will increase your visibility and in a passive posture, that is a sure give away.
5. The position should be pre-stocked, preferably with more supplies than a normal position if possible.

If your group can support a 24x7 over watch, this is a very powerful benefit in many of our ratings. This capability could eliminate the need for several Area Denial Systems and Early Watch Systems with a single solution. A good marksman, with night vision and a 360 degree view with powerful optics can be a complete game changer.

Even if the position cannot be manned 24x7, it can still be a potent fighting position. The benefits of an over watch position are so strong that if your location supports one, you should change some of the ratings on your worksheet.

 IF YOU HAVE A STRONG OVER WATCH, YOU SHOULD INCREASE THE HIGH GROUND RATING FOR YOUR LOCATION TO THE APPROPRIATE VALUE. IN THE DEFENSIVE EMPLACEMENTS SECTION, YOU SHOULD ALSO ENTER THE NUMBER OF OVER WATCH POSITIONS.

In summary, good cover is what is important for exterior positions. Trees, cars and a lot of other items in your yard are **NOT GOOD COVER**. Proper exterior positions can be accomplished without making your yard look like Fort Apache or lowering the value of your residence. One thing you should keep in mind is that you may have to fall back from your exterior positions. They will most likely not be pre-stocked, so your supply of ammunition, water and other items will be limited to what you carried there with you (see Load Vests ahead). If you are falling back, that means any attackers are probably moving forward. They may use your nice, well-made exterior positions against you. In most cases, this risk is worth it.

Windows will be the primary interior positions in any home. There are more of them than doorways and most of us don't want to cut through the walls. As stated above, the walls of homes are not bullet proof, so we must reinforce our interior positions.

External landscaping can be used as bullet stops if properly applied. It is common to use railroad ties, landscaping rocks and even pre-fabricated bricks around external areas. As described in section 6.12, the two keys to making this type of reinforcement effective:

1. The material or structure used must stop bullets.
2. The height of the barrier must allow for proper angles.

Normal rules about drainage also have to apply as we do not want to harm the value or appearance of our property.

As a general rule, ten or more inches of dirt will stop most rounds, especially if you have the barrier of your location's wall in addition to the dirt. Any wood or stone border reduces the thickness required.

This type of bullet shield does not have to be right up against your exterior wall. It can be landscaping "islands" some distance away from your structure.

Another option for exterior reinforcement would be portable potted plants. You should use non-ceramic pots as those may shatter with a single bullet strike. Plastic pots will take much more abuse. Potted plants have numerous advantages in that you can arrange them post-event if necessary. Rain water barrels will provide some protection as well, but these should be in a non-visible area (reference An Overgrown Mess – Section 6.10).

If your position is on the 2nd story or higher, then you need to reinforce the floor as well. Remember, <u>walls do not stop bullets</u> and the floor below you may not either.

If you have multiple windows, or a position that is intended to cover multiple windows, then you just need to build a bigger wall of sand. A bay window makes a great position concerning angles, but requires a lot of sand bags to reinforce. Notice the height that the glass begins off of the floor.

You also need to make the position a horseshoe shape if at all possible. It will probably end up that way by default for the simple reason of support.

Figure 35 - Window Above Floor Level

Count the number of Fighting Positions you have set up and enter them into the worksheet cell labeled "Fighting Positions." Unless you are simply modeling to justify the cost, don't count them unless all of the materials are ready including the pre-positioned supplies.

Note: When considering windows, you should know of a practice taught to entry or breaching teams called "**Break and Rake.**" Basically, in a non-hostage situation, a strategic window is broken and the inside of the structure is "raked" with fire. This clears the area for the team to enter through that window. Other than securing the window with plywood or burglar bars, there is little defense against this method. In violent locations, such as Rhodesia, grenade screens are a common security feature. Most of us do not want to put burglar bars or grenade screens on our windows, so the best option is to reinforce our positions so that they provide cover from this potential. Making your sandbagged area in a horseshoe shape will provide some measure of protection. You can also reference the information about cargo nets.

6.12.7   Key Placement of Weapons Systems

While this sounds all formal and scientific, it is actually a very simple part of your plan. Since we have already discussed angles and fighting positions, where you put your hardware is very simple.

The long range weapons should be as high as possible, perhaps on a second story window. If your location is single story, then this weapon should cover the most likely approach with the longest field of fire.

Medium range weapons should be prioritized to have the fastest shooting (normally the gun that holds the most rounds) covering the most likely approach.

Every shooter should have a *secondary* (pistol) on their person or at their fighting position.

What is the most important aspect of weapons placement is the distribution of firepower. As discussed before, the most likely method of attack you will experience is an enveloping attack, or an assault from more than one direction. While you may have taken every step possible to make your location invisible, once you are discovered, you don't know what direction(s) the assault is going to come from. If you can cover more than one direction, that is a positive. If you can move from one side to another to reinforce, that is even better and it greatly increases your chances of holding your location.

One of the greatest siege defenses ever recorded was the defense of *Bastogne* during WWII. Basically, the town was surrounded by the German Army that greatly outnumbered the U.S. Army defenders. Bastogne should have fallen easily given the size and condition of the defending forces, but they held in what many consider one of the most heroic efforts in U.S. Army history. While the bravery and effort of the individual defenders (101st Airborne) should not be forgotten, they also had an excellent defensive plan. Bastogne held, and is considered an important aspect in the failure of the German Army during the Battle of the Bulge.

A "defensive perimeter" was formed around the town. This is basically just a ring of defenses surrounding the town. In the center of the circle, they kept what is called a "Quick Reaction Force" or QRF, which is appropriately named. The QRF was fairly mobile group of men and equipment that could reinforce anywhere on the perimeter quickly. The Germans performed enveloping attacks. When the perimeter forces realized where the Germans were attacking in strength, they would release their quick reaction force to the location under stress. The Germans would believe they had attacked the strongest part of the perimeter and back off to try a different point. As soon as the attack died down, the QRF would go back to the center of the perimeter and wait for the Germans to hit another point.

You can do the same exact thing in the defense of your location. Let's take a simple, square layout and position our defenders. This is illustrated in the next diagram.

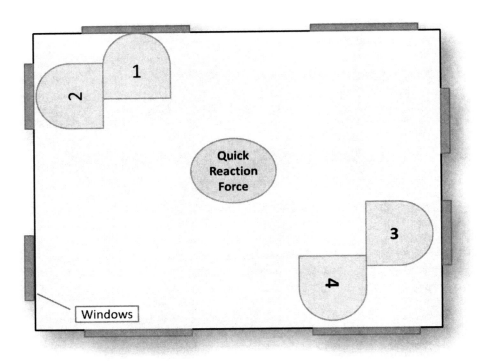

Figure 36 - Fighting Position Placement

Positions 1-4 are where our defenders are positioned. They have multiple angles of fire from reinforced positions.

With the above configuration, position 1 can reinforce 2 quickly. The number 3 can help 4 quickly and the Quick Reaction Force can make it to any if needed. In a real home, there are walls, furniture and other items in the way of communication and movement, so where you place the QRF is very important.

Combat veterans will also tell you that communication is critical in a gunfight. Can 1/2 hear 3/4 shouting? Can the QRF hear everybody? The best forms of communication during a gunfight are simple, practiced statements shouted loudly and clearly. Imagine you are the QRF and you need to determine which position to help and when. You are well aware that the attackers may be performing a feint or probe to determine your strong and weak points, so you can't go help at the first sign of trouble.

Position 1: "I have contact...I have contact....count 4 targets, armed, approaching slowly"

Position 2: "I have movement....I have movement"

Position 1: "Engaging"

Remember, gun fire is LOUD, especially in an enclosed area. The sound of the gunfire, combined with ear protection and the excited confusion of the fight demands clear, loud communications. Some phrases you might want to define and teach everyone would be:

- o **Contact** – this means I see bad guys or potential targets (Tangos)
- o **Movement** – this means I can see something moving, but can't tell what it is
- o **Engaging** – this means I am going to start shooting at them
- o **Receiving** – this means they are shooting at me
- o **Ammo** – means I need ammo
- o **Weapon Down** – means my rifle won't work
- o **I'm Hit, I'm Hit** (Help! Help! Or Medic! Medic!) – means I have been shot
- o Etc.

You can create your own phrases and words – there really are very few standard "pro words." As long as everyone understands them, they should work just fine.

Another important aspect for the QRF to judge is the rate of fire. The QRF should be the most experienced fighter or the person you judge to be the coolest head. They should know what sound each weapon or weapon type makes. They should know who has which weapon. If they hear heavy fire coming from 1 and 2, while 3 and 4 are silent and have reported no contact, it may be time to move to help 1 and 2. If everyone has contact and is firing, the rate of fire may be an indication.

6.13 Pre-positioning of Supplies

A big advantage for the defensive position is the pre-stocking, or pre-positioning of supplies. For our fighting positions, we can have water, ammo, tools and medical supplies already there. Any attacker has to carry everything they need for the fight on their backs and that slows them down. A modern day military assaulter carries 8-12 magazines on a chest rig. This is about 300 rounds. In addition, they carry water, a med kit, knife, radio, body armor and a variety of other equipment. It is not unusual for all of this gear and weapon to weigh 80 lbs. That will slow down anyone and limits their movements. Attacking takes a lot of energy and requires excellent physical condition.

Figure 37 - Example of a Chest Rig or Load Bearing Device

You, on the other hand, do not have to carry all of that, nor do you have to move as much. While I recommend everyone have a chest rig or other load bearing vest (see Fallback and Egress) during a gunfight, you can carry far, far less than the attackers.

The length of time an attacker can stay in the fight is directly dependent on how much weight they carry. When their ammo is depleted, they have to resupply. Chances are that resupply will be some distance from the fight.

So we, in order to prepare for the creation of firing positions, need a good list of what each position needs.

It is also important to remember that these are not just spots from which we will fight. We will be using these for observation and may be occupying the position for an extended period of time. Here is a list of what I plan to equip each of my positions with:

- At least 500 rounds of every type of ammo we will be using.
- Water
- Energy bars or similar quick food
- Eye protection
- Ear protection
- Weapon repair tools (normally a flat bladed screw driver and a cleaning kit)
- Tweezers
- Medical Kit
- Binoculars
- Flashlight
- Spare batteries for flashlights and optics (if required)
- Mirrors
- Duct tape
- Smoke Grenades
- Radio (if being used at the location)
- Towels and something to clean glasses/optics

I keep large plastic containers purchased at an office supply store for this very purpose. Each one has an inventory list printed and taped to the side.

If the Event occurs, I can pack each one and move it to my potential fighting positions.

My chest rig (load vest) is always packed because I use it to practice or when attending training classes. I keep it in an Army Surplus duffle bag and it is always ready to go.

Figure 38 – My wife loves it when I am sorting and preparing for TEOTWAWKI on the dining room table.

One of the most difficult tasks to perform under stress is the reloading of rifle magazines. A quality AR15 magazine can be purchased for about $15.00. While one or two of these are not a significant investment for most, having 20-30 of them in inventory causes problems with our methodology, since they would have no "dual use" for the average prepper. You should, however, keep in mind the egress or fallback potential, as there is no more efficient way to move large amounts of ammunition than pre-loaded magazines carried in load vest pouches.

There are a few quality "speed loading" devices on the market that really work. My favorite is from a company called LULU. I have heard good things about others as well. Having a device like a speed loader in your kit should be a consideration.

I am often asked "how much ammo should I keep in stock" and this is a difficult question to answer.

I reload my own, so the expense is not as great as if I were purchasing off of the shelf. I also believe that if an Event ever occurs, **ammunition will be THE item to barter with**.

As of this writing, 1,000 rounds of quality fighting ammunition for an AR15 platform will run close to $500 or more. Practice rounds can be found for $300 per 1,000 count cases. THAT IS A LOT OF MONEY.

My answer to the "how much" question normally ends up "as much as you can afford", which is often not much help. At minimum, I would have 1,000 rounds per defender of rifle ammunition and 200 rounds for each pistol. I keep 5,000 rounds per rifle shooter and 1,000 rounds for each pistol. I also keep a stock of .22 rounds for small game hunting and 1,000 rounds of shotgun shells.

Note: The storage of ammunition would seem a simple enough task. When you get into large quantities of stored munitions, it can be a bit of a pain. I used to use surplus ammo boxes purchased at around $10.00 each. The problem becomes apparent when you have dozens on them, with multiple calibers and a constant in and out of shooting, reloading and new purchases.

I finally stopped with the green metal ammo boxes and went with plastic storage bins. They are cheaper, lighter and I can see through them so as to tell how full and what caliber each is. They also stack better.

Figure 39 - Ammunition Storage Options

6.14 Fallback or Egress

I often refer to a location that is being prepared as "the Alamo" or "your Alamo." I am not referring to a rental car. For those not familiar with history, the Alamo was a fort in San Antonio, Texas where a bunch of folks set up a defensive location. While this is not a history book, and there are plenty of sources of information about the Battle of the Alamo, there is one VERY IMPORTANT historical fact that everyone should know. Most[8] of the defenders **DIED** there.

Most of us are all about duty, honor, sacrifice and valor – but quite frankly, I would prefer to live. I have a family that needs me. I need all of them. After all, the primary reason why most of us prepare in the first place is – **TO LIVE**.

History is full of examples where the defenders of castles, forts, firebases or other fixed locations were all killed in the effort. The main reason why this has happened is they were unable to retreat, fallback, escape or egress. Either there was no plan, or the enemy took away the option.

About now, some of the alpha-males start being uncomfortable with "retreat." Let me tell you sir, if two M1A1 Abrahams main battle tanks are rolling on your farm house – you better get your brave ass out of there and in a hurry because you are going to lose – PERIOD. I know this is an exaggeration, but the point remains – against overwhelming odds, I would prefer to execute an orderly retreat and fight another day.

There are two important concepts in retreat or fallback:

> **Breaking Contact** – This is actually a topic that the military spends a lot of time training soldiers on. There is a right way and a wrong way to do it. The primary goal of breaking contact is to "get away" without your pursuers being able to follow close enough to hurt you. This is typically performed in a manner that "buys time" for others. If you can slow the pursuit to a pace slower than your own, you gain distance, which is time and often, life. When breaking contact, the military teaches you to hinder the visibility of the pursuit and limit their capability to move forward. As an example, a smoke grenade or smoke device is a great way to limit their visibility. As far as hindering their ability to move forward, a concept called "bounding" is easy to practice and use.

> I won't go into a detailed description of bounding (sometimes called "buddy rushing" or "rushing") because there are several sources[9] where you can read and learn about basic "infantry maneuvers" and the proper way to do things if you feel it necessary. Bounding is very much like the game of leap-frog some children play, except you don't jump over each other's back. Instead,

---

[8] Of the Texans who fought during the battle, only two survived: Travis's slave, Joe, was assumed to be a noncombatant, and Brigido Guerrero, who had deserted the Mexican Army several months before, and convinced Mexican soldiers that he had been taken prisoner by the Texans.
[9] www.globalsecurity.org is a great free source for Military Field Manuals. Army Surplus stores also sell the actual hard copies for a few dollars.

you rotate who is covering while the other person moves (bounds) to the next position, alternating who moves. While one person is moving, the other has taken a knee or cover and is ready to fire. This process repeats itself over and over until it is unnecessary. Someone is always covering the direction (forward or to the rear) that you are moving from and/or too. I taught my son proper bounding movements in about one hour, but we practiced it for a long time before loading the weapons. Doing it wrong is an easy way to get hurt. ***Caution – don't load your rifles until you are sure you both understand the concept and angles of fire. Bounding requires muzzle discipline and takes practice.***

*Simple communications and capabilities, like bounding, can make all the difference in a fight. If I see my foe execute a proper bounding movement, I know they have skills and I may not follow them too closely. Know thy Enemy works both ways. There are several training schools, books and other sources (DVDs) that teach small unit communication and maneuvers. If you find that the members of your defensive group do not even know the basics, then you can always increase their knowledge and improve your plan. Bounding can be used to move **FORWARD** as well.*

The Rally Point. Another important concept of the escape is a rally point. This should be a pre-determined, backup location that is known by everyone. It is easy to get separated during a retreat and everyone should know where to "meet up." A typical rally point will be within one mile and in a relatively hidden position. An example would be "the railroad bridge" or "the old school house." If practical, emergency supplies should be pre-positioned at the rally point. If it supports hiding or burying some food, water, ammo or medical supplies, you will probably need them.

Depending on your location, you should initially plan the route(s) of the retreat. This can be as simple as a back gate, or a side door with good cover. It is unlikely that your attacker will have your place completely surrounded AND have enough force to overwhelm your defenses. While four people could "surround" the location, it should take those four plus several assaulters to push you out. That would probably be a very large group for a post-event world.

The decision, so I am told, on when to fallback is always a hard one. I would assume for our purposes it would be even more difficult. You have all of your shelter and supplies at your location. It is probably your home. You have prepared for years and now you are faced with being pushed out or overrun.

An officer with a lot of combat experience once told me, "The decision to bug out should be made when you still have the capabilities to succeed. You will know when it's time to go, just get out while you still can do it the right way. Don't wait too long trying to talk yourself out of it."

As stated above, bounding can be used to move forward, as well as a rear guard. The perfect retreat would be to have a team leading the egress, bounding out, the primary group (women and children) in the middle, followed by the rear guard exercising proper methods of breaking contact.

Everyone rushing out, all in a panic at the same time will lead to a rout. The attackers will have the momentum and your people could be hunted down and picked off one-by-one.

6.14.1   A Fighting BOB

Another important item to consider is the "bug out bag", or BOB. This is a little different BOB than what most of us normally consider when you include the chest rig. This is what we are going to grab on our way out in case the rally point stores are no longer there, or we are being pursued so closely we have to bypass them.

My actual BOB is very similar to what a lot of experts suggest you keep in a normal hurricane or earthquake bag. Ours are also used for camping trips. Here is a list of what I have, in a very good, custom fitted backpack. One is ready to go for each and every one of my defenders.

BOB Contents

1. **Fixed blade knife** – a hunting knife is a universal requirement. I like Gerber knives (about $100). I can't even begin to list the uses for a good knife. Forget the Rambo-esk survival knife.
2. **Multi-tool** – nothing fancy here. They are now cheap and like the hunting knife, they have a million uses.
3. **50 yards of 20lb test fishing line** – no, I am not going fishing unless necessary. Fishing line can be used to set tripwires (warning of someone approaching your camp), clothesline, hang food, close wounds, repair clothing, etc.
4. **1 roll of duct tape** – fix the tent, fix your clothes and close a wound. It also makes an excellent torch and is a great fire starter.
5. **3 king sized plastic yard trash bags** – you can make shelter, catch rain water, make a rain coat, etc.
6. **Camping stove** – the best I have ever seen is the German Army (yes, from WWII) stove. It is tiny, cheap and works. Get a few extra fuel pellets.
7. **Two Bic lighters** – stored so the gas does not leak out
8. **3 zip lock bags** – like the trash bags, they have a million and one uses.
9. **Water purifier** – I would not skimp on the Water Purifier. I went to REI and got a very good one. There are all kinds of options here depending on your budget and projected needs.
10. **Sleeping bag** – again, the military guys know their stuff here. I use a military grade ultra-light bag. You spend a little extra, but the reduced weight is well worth it.
11. **Baby wipes** – as many as I can carry. You would be shocked at how clean you can keep with a single baby wipe in the field. Get the unscented ones if possible.
12. **Inflatable sleeping pad**
13. **Towels**
14. **Dish washing soap**
15. **Personal hygiene:**
    a. Tooth brush
    b. Soap
    c. Razor
    d. Tooth paste
    e. Deodorant
16. **Tent** – I prefer small, 2-man tents. We are a family of four, so we have two 2-man tents. If one is damaged or lost, you still have a backup and can hot bunk it if necessary.
17. **Rain Parka** – make sure it is breathable and can fold up to a small package.

18. **Shovel** – I am talking about a camping shovel or military entrenching tool. You have to dig cat-holes in the wild. We once had to dig a drainage ditch around a campsite to keep the tents from flooding.
19. **Hatchet** – fire, and thus firewood is your friend.
20. **Steel drinking cup** – I like steel, because in a pinch, you can set in on the fire.
21. **Mess kit** – the army got it right here and it has remained unchanged for years. It works.
22. **Self-charging flashlight** – you know, the kind you shake and they charge.
23. **Food** – you don't have to purchase very expensive camping food. Most of it sucks anyway. On the other hand, canned food is heavy for the volume. A typical grocery store can stock your bug out bag pretty well. Don't forget the coffee, sugar, salt and pepper! The main thing to keep in mind is SHELF LIFE. The only specialized food we have is 3 military MRE (meals ready to eat) each, which you can purchase at most army surplus stores. Some ideas:
    a. Tuna in the foil pouch
    b. Dried beef
    c. Small peanut butter servings
    d. Dehydrated fruit
    e. Power bars and fruit bars
    f. Regular old Jell-O has more calories per oz. than just about anything with a decent shelf life.
24. **Water** – the best way to carry mobile water is called a 'camel back.' If you are not worried about being mobile, then just plain old bottled water works just great.
25. **Medical Kit**
    a. Tweezers
    b. EMT Scissors
    c. Normal assortment of bandages
    d. Sunscreen
    e. Anti-diarrhea medication
    f. Topical anti-biotic
    g. EPI Pens
    h. Any medication required by family
    i. Tape
    j. Alcohol or Sanitizer
    k. Aspirin
    l. Bug repellent
    m. Pain killers (left over prescription meds)
    n. Tampons (great to plug bullet wounds)
26. **Clothes** – we carry non-cotton shirts and pants. Even our socks are non-cotton. Cotton[10] should be avoided at all costs when considering clothing. The pants can double as swimming trunks and have removable legs (via zipper).
27. **Rope** or **Paracord** – I carry 50 ft. of 250lb rated nylon rope. It makes a great clothes line and has hundreds of uses. Don't forget to keep your food off of the ground.
28. **Maps**
29. **Compass**
30. **Whistle**
31. **Radios (2-way)**
32. **Machete**

---

[10] Most survival experts and extreme hikers avoid cotton because of its moisture retention. If you perspire, or get wet, cotton takes a long time to dry and this can cause problems with keeping warm.

All of this fits into a regular, quality backpack and essentially, we could survive most conditions for several days, if not weeks.

Also, if not camping in a state park, I would be wearing my "load vest" or chest rig, which has:

1. At least 3 full magazines of ammo (some guys think they have to carry 8 or more magazines, but I would prefer to save the weight/mobility in this situation)
2. Rifle maintenance kit and spares
3. Flashlight
4. Smoke Grenades
5. Medical Kit (more equipped towards combat wounds)
6. Knife
7. Pistol and Magazines
8. Night Vision Equipment

Even if we have to fallback from our defended location, we can hold our own.
Perhaps we will return and have a second go at our attackers.

There are many basic "movements", like bounding, that most of us don't think about on a daily basis. These may be valuable skills in a post-event world. Since we are focused on defense of a fixed location, I will not cover this topic in depth. I would, however, recommend that serious preppers take some time and at least read about how to execute these from professionals who have learned the "hard way." You may have to scavenge, hunt, trap or loot to survive and that means movement in a hostile environment. Good old Army field manuals are a great place to start, as well as DVD courses and training classes.

Everyone should know how to:

- "Pie" a doorway or entry
- Cross a street, open lane or stream
- Move through an urban area
- Maintain proper spacing while moving

Most of these capabilities are very simple and can save lives. You don't have to be as proficient as an infantry squad or a SWAT team to improve your chances in a bad situation. Just knowing the basics may help one day.

A few other items to consider about BOBs and a fallback or retreat:

- o I make sure every member of my group can carry their BOB and walk/hike a considerable distance. My wife has terrible knees, so she cannot carry as much as my teenage son. Make sure that everyone can carry their equipment. If you can't take a camping/hiking vacation, then put it on and go up and down some stairs.
- o We use ours for camping, so we know how everything works and why it is there. Every member of your group should know how to use all of the contents of your BOB as well. My daughter does not like weapons or gunfire, but she can load a magazine for all of the rifles and pistols.
- o My list includes several items that a soldier would consider frivolous and a waste of weight. I could not agree more for a soldier, but we, perhaps, just had to fall back from our "home", after a terrible fight. Morale can be improved by little things; like being able to brush your teeth, or washing your mess kit with soap.
- o We have redundancy on the critical items, such as a water purifier. You never know when someone will forget their bag on the way out or if it will be lost during the egress.

6.15 Spoiler Attacks

A spoiler attack is basically a well-timed "offensive" move against a foe who is preparing to attack your location. You "spoil" their fun, so-to-speak.

While our defense may be passive, if you know a gang is getting ready to attack your location, you can really ruin their day if you surprise them and hit first. Any attempt at a spoiler attack needs to be well thought out. The last thing you want to do right before being attacked is divide your forces; however, if you can catch them at the right time and place, a spoiler can be WELL WORTH THE RISK. Let's take a fictional scenario to show some examples on when a spoiler can be effective:

> *You are gathering firewood, and come across a group of armed men. They have not detected you. A leader is standing, giving orders to several others. You realize they are talking about YOUR location. You shoot the leader.*

In our little fantasy above, the right decision was easy because your forces (you) were already divided. It was also correct because you took out the leadership with little risk to yourself before their plan could even be communicated. As we stated above, our forefathers used the exact same tactic against the British during the Revolutionary War. You might as well hold up the tradition of the early American Rifleman.

Another scenario might be:

> *One of your group spots a bunch of men gathering for an attack. You decide to set up an ambush and take half of your defenders out to ambush them on the way to your location.*

This could be a VERY bad idea. You don't know the strength of the opposition. The men you spotted could be bait, with others already in ambush position. There are few military actions that are more devastating than a properly executed ambush, so you have to be SURE you are the one executing the action, not walking into one. Dividing your forces at this point is probably not wise.

Let's go over one more possibility:

> *You have a VERY good marksman in a high position. He spots a group of armed men heading directly for your location. Your location is the only reason for them to be heading towards you. He fires first, thus initiating the attack.*

A sniper (or any excellent marksman), is one of the most powerful assets on the modern battlefield. A single sniper can hold down dozens of men for hours, probably taking quite a few targets out of the fight. Few things can demoralize a group of soldiers more than being sniped. In our scenario above, this is a VERY potent Spoiler attack, not only for the people the sniper can eliminate from the attack, but also because the attacking force realizes they no longer hold the element of surprise. You take away their initiative and probably defeat the entire attack before it even gets started.

Even if you don't have a defender who is an accomplished marksman, you can still let the bad guys know they have been discovered and you send a message of – We are going to fight. Why don't you go find an easier target?

6.16 Area Denial Systems

Area Denial Systems (ADS) are devices or systems that discourage or prevent a foe from entering or using a specific area. Their primary purpose is to take options away from the bad guys. Area Denial Systems come in two basic flavors – lethal (anti-personnel) and non-lethal.

Examples of lethal systems would be mine fields, punji pits or booby traps. Examples of non-lethal systems would be tear gas, flood lights or thorn bushes planted in a defensive position.

As mentioned previously, lethal ADS are typically beyond the average prepper. They normally involve equipment or materials that are either illegal or VERY dangerous. If you are thinking about post-event options where you are not worried about a legal system (that no longer exists), these devices can still be very difficult or dangerous to make, deploy and maintain.

It is not uncommon for actions you take to reduce visibility to be in <u>direct contradiction</u> with ADS. If you park vehicles strategically to reduce visibility, you provide cover to anyone approaching your location. You would not be denying an area – you would be making it attractive.

Denial of an area to a potential attacker is, however, very effective and thus worthy of consideration. If you can eliminate one entire side of your location from potential attack, you don't need as many defenders on that side.

6.16.1   Lethal ADS

I have met many preppers who have complex plans for tripwires, homemade explosives, and electronic detonation triggers. Some of them have extensive training and education in explosives and related sciences and have a good chance of pulling it off. There are also powerful explosives in use daily at mines, construction and demolition companies, so they may be accessible to some individuals.

The average prepper does not have access to this type of equipment, nor do they have the proper skills to implement such devices safely.

I happen to reload my own ammunition, so I routinely access smokeless powder and primers. They are perfectly legal almost anywhere in the USA. So why couldn't I build my own Area Denial Systems? The first reason is that smokeless is not that powerful. It is widely published that modern plastic explosives are over 100 times more powerful than the average smokeless. It does not take an advanced degree in mathematics to conclude that a smokeless powder based hand grenade would have to weigh several times more than a modern military model in order to have the same limited effect. Unless you are a very big person, that weight does not work for throwing it very far.

There have been recent cases where "pipe bombs" have been effective against people. The Atlanta Olympics comes to mind as over 100 people were injured and two killed by a pipe bomb. That bomb however, weighed over 40 pounds, had directional steel plates and used a much more powerful explosive than smokeless powder.

Many people have high regard for the infamous Molotov cocktail, which is basically a glass bottle half filled with gasoline and plugged with a rag. You set the rag on fire and throw the bottle. When it hits and breaks, it starts a fire. Since gasoline buns at a VERY high temperature, this device has been effective against fixed targets. A small burning pool of gasoline is not going to slow down most charging attackers. You can basically run right through it or around it since it is not a very large obstacle.

I prefer the non-lethal variety of ADS for several reasons:

1. I can't blow myself or one of my kids up by accident.
2. I don't have to worry about animals setting anything off by accident.
3. I can prepare and practice with non-lethal devices legally.
4. I don't think organized, highly trained military-like units of men are going to be my problem. I think roving bands of the desperate are going to be the issue, so non-lethal will be more effective than normal.

If you are an explosives expert, alone in a remote area or just have to have homemade Area Denial Systems of the lethal variety that is up to you. I will add just a few bits of wisdom for the lethal type of systems:

1. Smokeless powder does not produce enough shock wave to cause injury. Unlike "high" explosives, which can kill just from their shock wave, "low" explosives like smokeless powder need shrapnel or projectiles to do damage.

2. Whatever type of devices you make, make sure they are weather proof. I once ran across a gentleman who had some "homemade grenades." He had used a pyro-based fuse (from a fire cracker I think) in short lengths and planned to light and throw them. I asked if he could give me a demonstration and he said sure, as soon as it stops raining. The fuse won't burn when wet. I wonder if he thought the bad guys would not attack during a rain storm.

3. High winds can interfere with tripwires and other types of automatic detonation. I know a rancher who purchased some very nice game cameras. In my mind, I was thinking that the motion sensors and wireless communication capabilities made them an excellent Early Warning System. I asked him later how they worked and he said they were great except for all of the false alarms. It seems when the wind blew hard, the trees would sway, and that caused the motion sensors to go off. Later, I read a blog where a man was thinking of hooking similar cameras up to a Lethal ADS and I bet that was going to cause issues.

4. Whatever type of devices you make, make sure they don't damage your location as much as attackers. Directional or shaped charges are a science and require either a lot of testing or a lot of math. Even with the math, testing should be done or you may hurt yourself more than the bad guys.

Lethal ADS is easier to implement in an active defensive plan since we don't have to worry about anyone seeing our systems. As a matter of fact, we probably want it as visible as possible. Old, rusty rolls of barbwire with weeds growing around them may be a scene common to some farms, but a side yard in an urban neighborhood with stakes, barbwire and slit trenches will stand out. If the post-event environment is such that you decide to go to an active method, then make your ADS look as imposing as possible. String "fake" tripwires, overturn dirt, even spread some bones around in order to send a powerful message.

For non-lethal ADS, I like systems that don't degrade my location's value or interfere with pre-event activates. Remember the "do not harm" rule of our methodology. If you have one side of a location that has no windows and thus no way to observe without electrically driven cameras, then it would make sense to anyone who scouted the location to approach from that direction. There is no way they can be seen from inside the structure. A solution would be to plant thick rows of thorny hedges or cactus beds as ADS. If you think hedges are not effective, talk to some WWII vets that fought through hedge rows in France.

Figure 40 - Crawling or running through this would make me want to take a different approach.

Some Cactus is also edible and a source of water if you live in the South West. Almost any location in the US has native thorn or "sticker" bushes that are attractive as landscaping, but would be an effective area denial. This may actually increase the value of your real estate and you will not regret the effort in case the world remains a sane place.

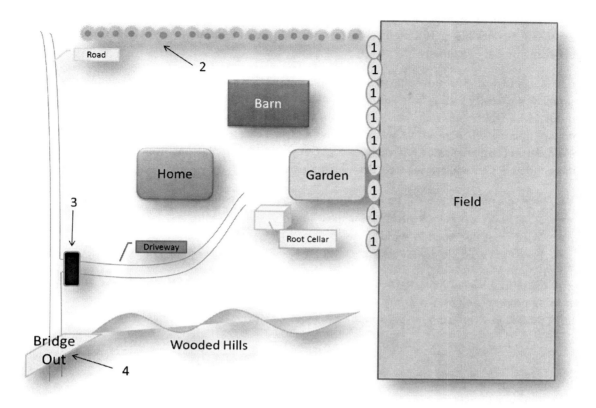

Figure 41 - Farm Location with Numbered ADS Options

Figure 41 shows our farm location with various non-lethal ADS implemented.

1. Our big, round hay bales that we used to reduce our Visibility Factor are also valid ADS.

2. We planted thick, thorny bushes along one edge of the property. If they are thick and close together, they become difficult to pass through, and thus would deny that area.

3. We parked one or more vehicles across the driveway.

4. We use some creativity to make the bridge appear to be out. This won't deny foot traffic, but may cause pause for any vehicles thinking of crossing.

A lot of people like flood lights, but I have mixed feelings about them. For an early warning, flood lights make sense to remove the element of surprise. Logically, you would think attackers would want to avoid a well lit area in favor of one that did not make them so exposed as targets. My biggest issue with this thinking is that they are only effective at night and I can shoot out the average flood light from over 200 meters away (I am an average shot). If you choose flood lights, use ones that have many smaller bulbs rather than just a few big ones. Count on the fact that they won't last long in a gunfight. If you have flood lights, then you have electricity.

The best way to determine how effective or feasible any ADS would be is to put yourself into the mind of an attacker, and really look at how you would "attack" your own location. If you use your imagination, you should see where and what ADS might make sense. Whether you are playing paint ball, Airsoft or at a military training school, every attack has to have a plan. There are just certain things that must be worked out and communicated to the assaulters. Get your team together and walk around your neighborhood or area and ask yourself the following questions:

- Where would I gather my people (departure or jump-off point)?
- What approach gives my people the most cover?
- What areas do I want to avoid?
- How am I going to deploy my men?

One of the most difficult things to overcome in this sort of exercise is that 99% of us have grown up respecting property and have a strong aversion to destroying things. In a post-event scenario, I don't believe the bad guys are going to give a rat's ass about your privacy fence or flower beds.

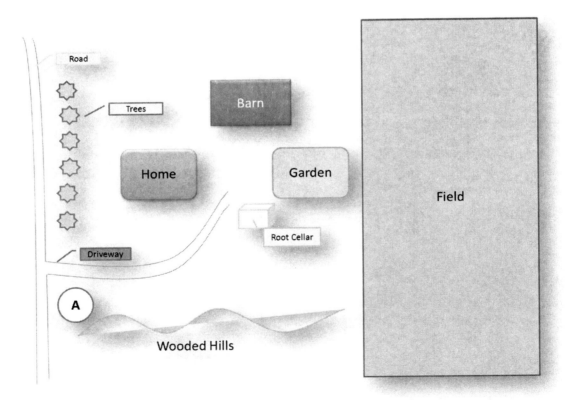

Figure 42 - Typical Farm Layout

Let's take an example of a typical layout. In Figure 42 we have trees between the road and our location, except for the area below the driveway.

I (the bad guy) have been scouting this home. I have watched you and know you are well armed. I don't like the idea of crossing your front yard on foot. It is too far and too exposed. I do like the idea of driving right up to the house and attacking that way. You have the driveway blocked, but there is an area (marked "A") that I can bypass your "roadblock." I also believe you have a lot of whatever I am after (probably food).

What if we simply planted a tree or two at Position A on the diagram? They don't even have to be big trees and it would take away my option of using my truck to knock a hole in your defense. Now I have to approach on foot. This is going to take time and I am exposed during the process. I have a reasonable chance of being discovered and losing my element of surprise. **Planting the trees would be an Area Denial System.**

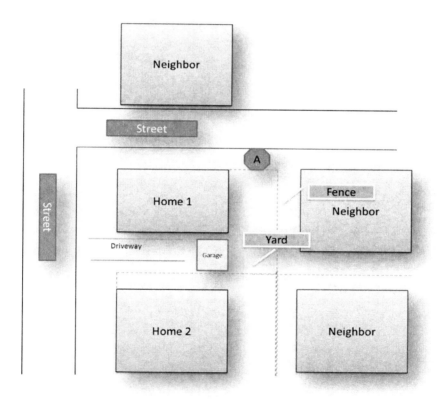

Figure 43 - Typical Suburban Layout

Let's take an example of a typical suburban neighborhood. In Figure 43 we have typical privacy fences surrounding the backyards. For Home 1, the street is very close and it is just 20 feet of yard between the curb and the fence marked as "A."

I (the bad guy) have been scouting this home. I have watched you and the neighbors talking and know you all are well armed and are probably helping each other. I also believe you have a lot of whatever I am after (probably food).

If I approach your house from the front street, I expose my back to the entire street. If I come at your house from the backyard, I now have the advantage of limited visibility from the neighbors. All I have to do is breach the fence from the street and my guys can pour in and surprise you. If I have a car/truck, I can just drive up from the street, push through the fence and come on in.

I could also pull up on the street, jump out and take out the fence and pour into the backyard. I have egress, my vehicle will provide me cover from the neighbor across the street (at my back) and once I take the house, I control an important location that I can use as a jump-off to take down the entire neighborhood.

Home 2 has none of these exposures.

What if we simply planted a tree or two at Position A on the diagram? Now I have to remove two or three boards to get in. I have a reasonable chance of being discovered and losing my element of surprise.

Planting the trees would be an Area Denial System.

Why not just jump the fence? Soldiers hate going over obstacles like a privacy fence. You are exposed while going over. You don't know what is on the other side and can't maneuver while you are throwing a leg over. It can also be difficult to do when you are holding a weapon and being weighed down with a lot of kit (gear). Ten out of ten times, I believe a looter would prefer a breach and go through with both feet on the ground as opposed to going over the top of a fence. If I, as the bad guy, was trying to sneak into your backyard, I would use a different method, but going over a fence would be my last resort.

When you think of area denial, you should not just think about your yard or the area around your location, but approaches to it.

In a rural setting, could you block the road some distance from your location and deny anything but dismounted (on foot) access? This would be area denial (and an effective one at that).

Can you use our Hollywood façade techniques to make a bridge look like it is out? This would be area denial.

Heavy brush piles, damned up creeks and lots of other options can deny the bad guys access to your location. It can force them into routes that you can see better, have early warning in place or simply make them go elsewhere.

Bamboo, if it grows in your region, makes a great ADS. It grows quickly and can get very tall (Visibility Factor). While the individual plants are not much trouble, a thick row of them would require a machete to breach. Anything that takes the attacker a while to "hack" through will be a deterrent. If you choose bamboo, don't forget to string a tripwire EWS through it just in case.

Security gates are another form of ADS. It is not unusual to see a suburban home with an iron gate across an entry way or front door. If properly secured, it can take time to breach and time is the friend of the defender, the enemy of the attacker.

Cargo nets can be used as ADS internally. They are one of my favorite ways to secure the inside of a bank of windows or double door. If you secure them in multiple places, with hooks into a stud or doorframe, they can be a real problem for someone trying to enter. While they could eventually be cut out of the way, that takes time. You can see and shoot through them and they let in light. You can remove them (from the inside) with little effort.

NOTE: There is a certain amount of physics involved in breaching and denial of breaching. Most doors are secured by 4 or 5 "points" - n locks plus three hinges. Remove one side of these points and the door fails. Put enough pressure on the door as a surface, and points will fail. The most effective method of securing a door is to have more "points" to absorb any force against it. It is even better if these points are flexible so as to absorb the energy being applied to the door. This is similar to how a bullet proof vest "disperses" energy from a single point (the bullet) across a wide area. If you secure a door with netting, it will have dozens of points (the hooks) to absorb and thus disperse the energy being applied against the door. It may fly off the hinges, but the netting will keep it affectively "in place." If the net is tight enough, the door may be "hanging" in the net, but still blocking entry, and thus serving its purpose.

If you "plant" ADS or EWS, **MAKE A MAP**. I call this the "Easter Egg" syndrome. If you have ever had an Easter egg hunt with the kids, and a few weeks later smell something really bad only to find an undiscovered, rotten egg, then you understand. More importantly, you want to be able to check your ADS and EWS on a regular basis. You probably will have a lot on your mind, so a map will help you to remember.

As you consider any type of ADS, you should enter the potential results in the worksheet values for open access, limited access and no access. These values have a considerable impact on the location rating, so Be conservative with any assumptions. Obviously any direction that is denied to a potential foe gives the defenders an advantage. The fewer directions you have to cover MEANS MORE focus on the remaining open DIRECTIONS.

7. The Perimeter

One of the most commonly used terms in war movies is "the perimeter." Perimeters are constantly being manned, breached, reinforced, over-run, probed, penetrated or simply patrolled.

What is a perimeter? It is one or more boundaries that enclose an area that is occupied or defended. It's a "line in the sand" that we draw, and say that is ours, or theirs. For our purposes, we will define three perimeters:

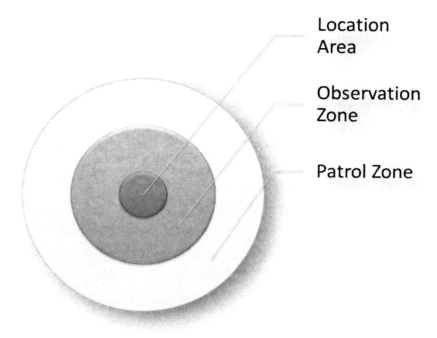

Location Area

Observation Zone

Patrol Zone

Figure 44 - Generalization of Perimeters with Primary Center Location

- The inner circle represents our Location Area that we have been using throughout the book. Its outer ring defines our Location Perimeter.
- The middle circle is the area surrounding our Location Area. We should be able to observe almost any level of threatening activity within it. We will call this the Observation Zone, and its outer ring is the Observation Perimeter.
- The outer circle is our Patrol Zone, and its outer ring is the Patrol Perimeter.

Don't worry, I am not going to recommend heavy foot patrols nor will I attempt to persuade you to build 20 foot high earthen works around each ring. We will have activity and options in each of these three areas that, when combined, are a significant part of our plan.

The size of each area, and thus its perimeter, depends on the size of your Location Area, the surrounding terrain and the type of defense you plan to implement (active or passive).

The primary activity in each area will be:

Patrol Zone – Walk or drive this area as often as possible. What you are looking for is any sign that your location is being scouted or observed. Try to find any position that can see or observe your Location Area and look for any signs that someone is using that position to watch you.

Observation Zone – This is the perimeter that you can keep scouted or keep under watch. In an urban area, this may be restricted to just a few blocks or less. If you have a two story home, your Observation Zone would be larger than a single story home.

Location Area – this is the same area that we have been using throughout the book. This is your yard, garden, barn, outbuildings, lake, or any other places you will need to operate in on a daily basis.

Our objective is to **CONTROL** the Observation Zone and Location Area, if at all possible. That ground is ours to hold and keep. The Patrol Area is "no man's land", or a buffer zone for our inner perimeters.

If you have a large group of defenders, then you will probably have the luxury of someone being on constant "guard duty" or observing your perimeters to make sure no one sneaks up and surprises you. If your group of defenders is smaller, then you are probably going to be spending a majority of your time just getting enough food, let alone patrolling some line in the sand looking for trouble.

Regardless of the size of your group, there are a few basic "rules" that we will use as we prepare our perimeters in the following sections:

1. Your defenses should become stronger as the enemy moves from outer to inner rings.
2. Your observation capabilities should increase as the enemy moves from outer to inner rings.
3. Your Early Warning Systems should become denser as the inner ring is approached.
4. Your ADS should become more effective as the enemy approaches from outer to inner rings.

While this sounds logical, you would be surprised at how many preppers spread their limited defensive capabilities over two wide of an area. They have early warning systems, like tripwires, spread all over their Patrol Perimeter and nothing in the observation area.

As we go through the following sections, we will refer back to the names of these perimeters and zones for reference. The primary reason why you should define perimeters is for communication between your group members.

It could be very important for everyone in your group to know what "get the children inside of the location" means. Another example would be "Dad, I just saw two men walking down the street. They are inside our Observation Zone." Finally, consider "Bill and Tom, grab your rifles and go check out the northern Observation Perimeter."

You can name your zones and perimeters anything that makes sense to you and your group. The name is not important (but should make sense). It is the description and commonly understood or agreed upon meaning that is critical.

7.1 Range Cards

If your group has the advantage of having one or more snipers or long range marksmen, one of the best preparation actions you can do is to create a range card.

If your location does not have visibility beyond 200 meters or so, then a range card is not going to do you any good. The same applies if you don't have any long distance shooters in your group.

A range card is a simple map of the area around your location with various landmarks drawn and the distance (range) from a fighting position to that landmark.

If you are, or have serious hunters (or golfers) in your group, they probably have a laser range finder. This device gives very accurate distance measurements when pointed at a target. You can use this device or simply "walk it off" to measure the distance to certain objects from your fighting positions.

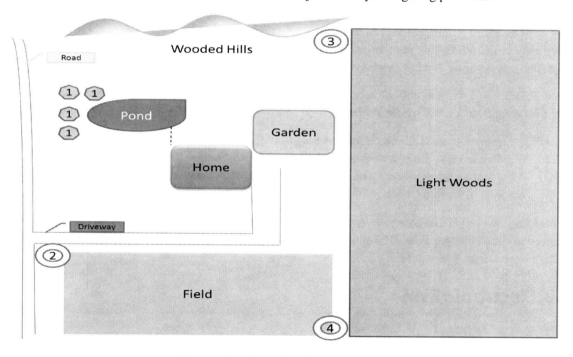

Figure 45 - Example of a Range Card

1. Far Tree is 310 meters.
2. Mailbox is 330 meters.
3. Big Oak is 410 meters.
4. Gate is 615 meters.

This is important, because bullets do NOT go in a straight line – they drop and spin off-line. As an example, the average AR15 bullet will drop over 20 inches at 400 meters. At 600 meters, it drops over 70 inches. Long range shooters will know the ballistics of their weapons and ammo. They will understand the drop, spin and other factors that affect THE SHOT. What is critical to them is the DISTANCE.

Snipers, when they get to their desired position, will "laz" (laser range) various objects or landmarks and make a range card. When their target is next to one of those objects, they know the range, and thus the corrections to make to their aim in order to hit their target.

Since we are defending a fixed position, it will save a lot of time to have these distances pre-determined and will also give you a realistic indication of your perimeters, zones and warning times.

7.2 Early Warning Systems (EWS)

Practically nothing provides an attacker with more advantage than the element of SURPRISE. A military unit in the field utilizes a significant percentage of their resources to avoid being surprised. Unfortunately for most of us, our resources in a post-event defense will probably be limited at best. Unless you have a very large and well trained group, you will not be able to afford the luxury of having people on constant guard duty or patrolling your perimeters. Let's be realistic here, you will probably be spending most of your time just ensuring you have enough food and water.

For our purposes, I will categorize Early Warning Systems (EWS) into two types, electronic and manual. What we want from a EWS can be summarized as follows:

1. We want to know if anyone is approaching our location.
2. We want to know from which direction they are approaching.
3. We want this information without constant false alarms from wildlife or weather.
4. We want to know as much information about the approaching people as possible.

In summary, we want to be able to sleep at night knowing that we will not wake up with the barbarians at the door of the Keep. We want to be able to utilize our resources and people to make life better, not performing constant guard duty.

7.3 Electronic EWS

If your location is going to have a constant source of electricity, then you have an enormous advantage. The capability to recharge batteries, power a computer and other devices is invaluable.

Game Cameras are amazing devices and relatively inexpensive for the amount of security they provide. They are robust, weather proof and easily hidden. You can even purchase infrared models for a few dollars more. If you have a reliable source of electric energy, then you can set up a series of game cameras that will "report back" to your PC via a wireless link. No need for a network, the internet or

Figure 46 - Camo Game Camera

any service other than what you can control. Your PC can then sound an alarm when activity is detected by one of the cams. As of this writing, I could provide 360 degree coverage for almost any location for less than $2,000, not counting the computer. Prices continue to decline.

When the game camera detects motion[11], it basically takes a picture and then transmits that picture to the computer. You can view the picture and know which camera it was taken from. If it was a dog, or a deer, then you can relax. If it was three guys carrying AK47s then you have an advantage immediately.

Perimeter Lasers can be purchased from several different sources. They basically shoot a laser beam in a straight line and when someone or something "breaks" the beam, an alarm is sounded. Perimeter lasers are small, easy to hide and relatively weatherproof. The problem is false alarms and a lack of information about what tripped the alarm. Dogs, deer, feral hogs or other large animals can trip the alarm and you are going to have to go check it out. After a while, if it continues to "cry wolf", you may not even bother and that could be dangerous.

Figure 47 - Perimeter Lasers

I like perimeter lasers for privacy fences and other narrow locations that wild animals would typically avoid. If you mount a laser along your backyard fence, about one foot from the top and one foot from the fence, you will catch anyone coming over or through the fence. A quality perimeter laser system can be purchased from almost any home security store or from several sources on the internet. You can even purchase solar powered units, but these would be a little harder to hide. You can equip a very large perimeter for less than $1,000.

Security cameras are commonly used by office buildings and other industrial locations, but they normally require constant monitoring. Some systems do incorporate motion detection and this might be a viable option for your location. As the capabilities of these systems increase, as in weatherproofing, motion detection, range, and wireless communication, so does the price.

There are also vibration sensing devices, radar and microwave based devices, but these are VERY expensive and require specialized training to install, maintain and use. I consider these to be out of reach for the typical prepper.

---

[11] Beware of mounting game cameras where wind can cause false alarms. Infrared units are less susceptible to this problem.

7.4 Manual EWS

The most common and probably most effective warning system is a dog. Man's best friend has better ears and nose than we do and the typical "watch dog" will detect someone approaching long before a human will. The problem with watch dogs is that we need an "early" warning system and a dog's range of detection is probably less than 150 meters. They are great for patrolling though, if properly trained.

Another traditional form of EWS is the watchtower sentry. Sentries have been effective for thousands of years. If you have the manpower and the location, a sentry routine may be a good choice. There are serious issues with sentry duty and watchtowers. First of all, it is about the most boring task you could give to anyone. Police officers hate "stakeouts" because of the hours of tedious observation. Standing guard duty is worse and staying "frosty" is going to be difficult. The second primary issue is that a watchtower, to be effective, has to be able to see for long distances. It, in reverse, can be seen from long distances. If you are going with a passive defense, this is not a good thing. If your location and manpower allows for a watchtower, the most important aspect is the alarm. Set up a bell, air horn, whistle, gun, or some other means to send the signal that someone is approaching.

Any type of EWS that does not require electrical power should be considered manual. The primary example of a manual EWS would be the infamous "tripwire." Tripwires have been used for thousands of years and can be very effective. In military circles, the tripwire is almost exclusively used for "booby traps" or other lethal devices (see Area Denial Systems), although the concept is practically identical for "trip flares" or "trip alarms."

There are two parts to a tripwire – the actual **wire**, or triggering device, and the **alarm**, or signal.

One of the most commonly known setups for a tripwire is a metal can with pebbles inside and a string tied around it. The string (tripwire) is tightly pulled across an area and anyone or anything that passes through that area will hit the string (*wire*) and cause the can (*the alarm*) to fall making a noise.

While in theory this sounds great, making a good tripwire EWS is **NOT** that simple. First of all, you have weather to deal with. Any EWS should be capable of withstanding wind, rain, snow, ice and other exposed conditions. With our example of the can, the first good wind that comes along could blow it over.

The second problem with a tripwire is discovery. American troops in Iraq use "silly string" and spray a shot of string across an area they are concerned about. If the string hits the ground, all is clear. If not, they know EXACTLY where the tripwire is. For our purposes, we have a major failure if the bad guys discover our tripwires. First, an area we counted as being secured with warning device has now been breached. Second, the bad guys know that **someone** set that tripwire for **a reason**.

There are methods that can be used to increase the effectiveness of tripwires. First of all, the type of wire being used is critical. The two most common choices are lightweight fishing line and ultra-thin gauge copper wire. Both of these have their issues. Fishing line, for example, is VERY visible in direct sun light. Copper wire has less flexibility and is more visible in general than clear fishing line. The type of line you use should depend on the location and its lighting.

I prefer the indirect method of using tripwires. For example, we want to have EWS on a narrow area between a barn and a privacy fence (Figure 48). The area, as shown below, is about 8 feet wide. A tripwire would easily be seen and avoided. What would not be so easy to avoid is a tree limb or other natural looking piece of debris that could easily be moved by someone trying to sneak through that passage. You can simply attach the tripwire to an obscure point on the debris and when it is moved, the alarm is sounded.

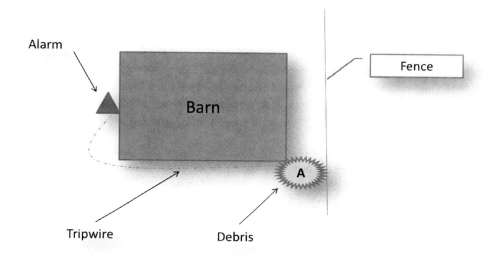

Figure 48 - Potential Manual EWS Location

Some other examples of indirect tripwires would be:

- String a tripwire through shrubbery that is not dense enough to prevent passage.
- Windowsills and behind closed doors (on the inside) make great places for tripwires.
- Low hanging tree branches that would have to be moved in order to pass.
- A loose board or a wobbly rail on a bridge.
- A loose horizontal board on a fence that falls when someone tries to cross.
- Loose wire on a fence.
- A fence post, such as on a barbwire fence, that is set badly on purpose with a tripwire attached.

Good places to hide direct tripwires:

- At the bottom of steep inclines where anyone coming down would be moving quickly and not have time to look for tripwires.
- Leaf piles are great at hiding tripwires as long as the wind does not blow your cover away.
- Fence lines with high weed growth. Beware of cattle or other animals that can trip them.
- Soft sand makes a great place to hide tripwires. The wire typically has to be tight enough to alarm if only stepped on rather than "tripped."

7.4.1 Tripwire Alarms

The alarm component of your tripwire must be something that is unusual to get your attention. It must do so even while you are asleep. It must work day or night, in all weather conditions.

Sound is the most common alarm used in manual tripwire setups. Since we don't have electric alarms, buzzers or other indicators, sound is really the only sensory indicator that works all the time. That being said, it should be a loud, distinctive noise.

One of my favorite tripwire alarms is the common shotgun shell. They are weather proof, cheap, commonly available and make one heck of a noise that can be heard for a long distance. You can make blanks (or purchase them) without being an expert on reloading so as not to hurt livestock or children. You can purchase commercially available devices that when a wire, or string is pulled, the shell explodes. These are robust devices specifically made for tripwires.

You can also make your own, and they are perfectly legal in most states as long as they are not intended for anti-personnel use. With a little practice, you can create a tripwire alarm for less than a dollar including the 12 gauge shell.

1. Purchase blank 12 gauge shells. ***Do not attempt this with regular shells!***
2. Take a common mousetrap and drill a hole directly below the hammer (the part that kills the rodent) as shown below.

Figure 49 - Mouse Trap with Drilled Hole

Glue your blank shotgun shell (*an empty is shown in the photo for safety*) onto the back of the mousetrap with any waterproof glue. The primer of the shell should be centered on the drilled hole.

Figure 50 – Mouse Trap Alarm with Shotgun Shell Glued to Back

Now you should put on gloves and eye protection and then arm the trap carefully, and I do mean *carefully*.

Place a small block of wood over the drilled hole. This is to protect the shell from impact in case you mess up and trip the trap. **Carefully** attach the tripwire to the cheese tray. Once the wire is stable, remove the block of wood.

Gently slide a flathead nail or tack into the drilled hole. The nail should fit snug, but not too tight. **DO NOT FORCE THE NAIL INTO THE HOLE.**

Figure 51 - The Completed Tripwire Alarm. BE CAREFUL!

When the tripwire is pulled (tripped) it will pull the cheese tray and the hammer will snap onto the nail, driving it into the primer. **Boooom!**

*I **strongly suggest** that you practice this with spent shells the first few times. Be aware that the explosive force of a blank can **hurt** you badly or even kill.*

Several types of smoke grenades use a pulling motion to ignite them. These can be effective alarms in the daylight hours, but are difficult to detect at night.

Another source of alarm devices is a boating supply store. Every vessel over a certain length in U.S. waters must carry some number and type of signal flares. The most common signal flares are called "rocket" flares and can reach about 400 feet in height. At night, they are obvious, but during the day, if you are not looking in that general direction, you could miss the alarm.

Note: Marine supply stores also carry parachute flares, which will stay in the air for several minutes. The military has used flares to illuminate attackers for years. These will definitely work in lieu of night vision.

Anything that is loud and has a unique sound can be used as an alarm. Bells, magnetic door alarms (waterproofed), air horns and other such noise makers can all be configured to "engage" when a tripwire is pulled. The secret is to test, test and then test some more.

7.4.2 Considerations on EWS

For no other reason than Electronic EWS, you should consider the purchase of a limited power solar solution. Rechargeable batteries do not require a large power source and backpacking solar charging systems are not overly expensive. For the typical EWS, you are going to need at minimum the capability to recharge some batteries and perhaps, recharge your laptop computer.

You just can't beat the security the electronic devices provide.

I would still supplement any Electric EWS with manual devices. You never know when electrical devices will fail. You will also gain the experience to quickly "swap it out" in case your recharging system fails.

7.4.3 Placement of EWS

In Section 7, The Perimeter, we described three perimeters and their associated zones. The reason why we have EWS is to provide WARNING. How we can react to that warning determines where we should place our EWS. It is also an important factor in the size and configuration of our perimeters.

If you already have a preparation plan, you should have a general idea of what daily life will be. There will be chores and tasks associated with gathering and preparing food (gardening), maintenance of your location, hunting, gathering and care of dependents. Survival "honey do's" if you will. When the alarm is sounded, there should be a plan of action for all of the occupants of your location. This is who goes where, who is responsible for what and where everyone should be – **BATTLE STATIONS**. This applies to the middle of the night as well as the middle of the day.

What is important for our plan, and the EWS, is how long it will take to execute the "alarm plan." On a farm with a large Location Area, it could take some time before everyone reaches their assigned positions. In a suburban setting, it could be a matter of seconds.

Your EWS should provide you enough time to execute that plan. If your people are to man fighting positions, give them the time to get there. If your defenders need to "gear up" and take a position, then the EWS should be far enough away to provide the time to accomplish this.

HOWEVER, there is a big problem!

The typical person can walk at five miles per hour, and I think this is a safe assumption for our plan. Any attackers would be carrying weapons and some amount of water and gear, so even if they started "double timing" after THEY heard your alarm, you should be safe calculating with that speed. That means they will travel 150 yards (125 meters), or 1.5 football fields in one minute.

When I first calculated this, I realized that we simply did not have enough time to execute our plan. I had planned for my EWS to be about 600 yards away, and there was no way we were going to be ready to "repel borders" in less than five minutes.

About now, you begin to understand why when the alarm is sounded for BATTLE STATIONS in the movies, all of the soldiers and sailors rush around like crazy to get to their positions. You might think, "Why don't you just move the EWS farther away"? The problem then becomes one of geographical area. The further you move the EWS away from the central point of your location, the area requiring EWS grows exponentially.

An effective EWS can be implemented, but it is typically a compromise of very quick actions by your defenders and realistic distances of EWS installation.

It is also about now that most people that I refer to as "lone wolfs" begin to realize why there is security in numbers. It is easier to implement an effective defense with a larger number of people. This is perhaps why throughout our development as a civilization, we have always grouped together and organizations have formed. Scientists who study our social history refer to this as "division of labor." I can keep an armed watch while you harvest the squash.

After a while, you can drive yourself mad with all of this. It begins to seem impossible to live this way. It will most certainly require a large percentage of your time just for the basics of food, water and shelter. How can a small group perform these tasks and still "keep watch" through the night? You **MUST** sleep sometime.

This is the reason why military units have such extensive support and logistic capabilities. For every "rifle", there are 4-5 "behind them" providing support. You, as a prepper, probably won't have that luxury.

But don't give up. Most of security and defense is simply mindset with a little extra equipment. I carry a briefcase with a laptop computer for my normal job. If I, after a hectic morning, get to the car without it, my brain says "missing something", and I go back and get it.

In the post-event world, you may have to substitute that briefcase for a rifle and sling. You and your group, according to our Event Horizon (Figure 3), should have some time to adapt to this new "lifestyle." Regardless of the nature of a National Event, there will be a Grace and Realization Period where absolute awareness and security will not be critical.

I don't wear my chest-rig around the house all the time. You won't see my kids practicing storming the house with Airsoft guns. We don't take turns staying up throughout the night keeping "watch". Life is busy enough without adding the burden of preparing for something that is simply unlikely to happen.

What we do practice on is the very basics to make sure we can adapt later. Now and then, I take my children "to the country", away from any judgmental eyes, and we strap on some gear and "run around" the woods. They think it's like a real life video game.

Figure 52 - Old Picture of the Author's Son (that Load Vest looks a little big)

It is actually fun and gets them away from cell phones and that video game trap. My son, without any military training, would be an asset in any stressful situation.

7.4.4 Area Denial and EWS

Area Denial Systems (Section 6.16) and EWS should work hand-in-hand to provide:

- Fewer resources required to keep watch or for guard duty
- Mental security – everyone has to sleep some time
- Warnings of anyone approaching our location to avoid surprises

Your EWS positioning, combined with your Area Denial Systems should be integrated. The two combined should provide for enough warning for you and your group to react. Let's take some examples and see how we can implement EWS in order to enhance our security.

The diagram below (Figure 53) is our example from the section on reducing visibility. The numbered areas are examples of where we have implemented ADS are:

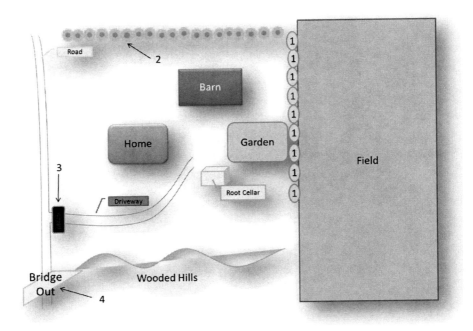

Figure 53 - Overview of a Farm with ADS (indicated by the numbers) Implemented

1. Our big, round hay bales that we used to reduce our Visibility Factor are also valid ADS.
2. We planted thick, thorny bushes along one edge of the property. If they are thick and close together, they become difficult to pass through, and thus would deny that area.
3. We parked one or more vehicles across the driveway.
4. We use some creativity to make the bridge appear to be out. This won't deny foot traffic, but may cause pause for any vehicles thinking of crossing.

We need to add some EWS to our example. The wooded hills, at the bottom of the diagram may reduce visibility, but also may be attractive as a jump-off point for raiders. So we will need to implement some sort of EWS in that area.

The front yard (between the home and the road) is also wide open.

While the large hay bales may be effective at reducing our Visibility Factor, and may allow limited ADS, they can provide cover for anyone who makes it across the field undetected.

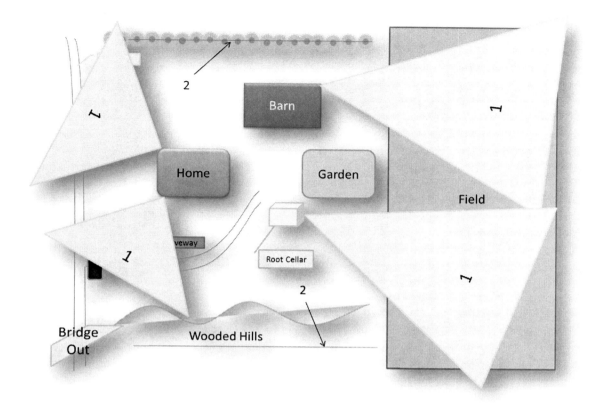

Figure 54 - Overview of the Farm, with EWS (numbered) Installed

Now we have added four game cameras (1), and two tripwires with alarms (2). Our farm has an excellent visibility factor, well-positioned ADS and effective EWS. In order to accomplish all of this, we would not impact the value of the property one single bit. As a matter of fact; we probably increased the value because of the landscaping if done properly. Our total investment for all of this would be less than $1500.

One of the most critical areas to consider for EWS or ADS would be a tree, rooftop or other "high" area that can be used to observe your location. My thinking is that EWS is the first priority in that we don't want anyone "up there" scouting. If it is a tree, remove the lower branches. If it is a rooftop, remove the fire escape ladder. Deny the spy access to the high ground. If an ADS is not practical, you may want to set up an EWS so that you know if someone is, or has been, up "there."

 WHILE ANY EWS DOES NOT TECHNICALLY PROHIBIT A FOE FROM ACCESSING YOUR LOCATION FROM A DIRECTION, IT DOES REMOVE THE ELEMENT OF SURPRISE. THE FACT THAT AN APPROACHING PARTY WOULD BE DETECTED AND CONFRONTED AT A DISTANCE IS ENOUGH FOR OUR WORKSHEET. FOR EACH DIRECTION THAT YOU INSTALL AN EWS, YOU COULD UPDATE THE LIMITED ACCESS COUNT AS WELL (IF THAT DIRECTION WAS ORIGINALLY COUNTED AS OPEN ACCESS). IN THE DEFENSIVE EMPLACEMENTS SECTION, YOU SHOULD UPDATE THE COUNT FOR **EWS DIRECTIONS**.

8. Safety in Numbers

By now, most people realize that performing security or defensive tasks is going to be time consuming and absorb a lot of resources. Even with EWS or ADS, being secure can be labor intensive. The best solution is to increase the number of people in your group.

The first option for "recruits" is typically family members. If you live close to them and they share your prepper mentality, then they would be an excellent addition to your group. While disagreements may arise over whose home is the better location to weather the storm, or other various matters, family members are typically known and trusted more than any other potential additions.

The second option is normally neighbors. Their geographic location alone (multiple angles and angles via group) makes them an excellent choice. While the concept of approaching neighbors may be uncomfortable, it can be done gracefully. I think you would be surprised at how many people think about their future if things go badly on a large scale.

The third option is friends. From the perspective of trust and similar ways of thinking, most people find that friends make the best additions to a forming group. The issue with a lot of friends is their geographic location. Will everyone be able to get to the Bug Out Location?

The fourth option is organizations or clubs. While your church may not be the best place to start a discussion of defensive planning for the post-apocalyptic world, your local VFW or similar organization might be.

Do not discount elderly people as solid contributors to any group. I once had a discussion with an elderly couple and their concerns about preparing. They were not as mobile as they once were and the eyes and ears were becoming an issue as well. I suggested that they approach some neighbors and see if anyone else shared their concerns and if so, join a group. "Who would want us? We would be such a burden" was their thinking. I told them that they had to make themselves "attractive" to a group. While their physical limitations were a negative, their skills, experience and heart were the most important factors. If there was a group in the neighborhood, they had to be lacking something – food stores, ammunition, or medical supplies – because prepper groups **NEVER** have enough. Could they babysit children? Help with the canning or sewing?

Regardless of age, skills or education, everyone in a group must contribute and most people have skills or talents that would be a positive contribution to any group. If all else fails, the sharing of the financial burden alone can make anyone a welcome member to some groups.

8.1 Weapons Training

One of the best ways to improve your Group Rating is with weapons training. While I do not mean to belittle other valuable survival skills, this is a book focused on defense.

While pistols are excellent for close quarter situations, the bulk of the work will probably be done with rifles. Chapter 11 describes the requirements for weapons in detail, but improvements in any skills with a rifle will increase the capability of your defense along with the confidence of your group.

While fighting with a rifle is a multifaceted skill set, there are two categories that will impact our defensive plan the most:

- o Advanced Rifle Skills
- o Long Range Marksman

8.1.1 Advanced Rifle Skills

My definition of advanced rifle skills is probably different from what the typical soldier would list. In my experience, the following skills would be considered "advanced":

1. The ability to rapidly engage targets out to 400 meters (440 yards) and have a greater than 50% hit rate within 200 meters on a man-sized target.
2. Being capable of changing magazines quickly and reliably.
3. The ability to clear typical malfunctions quickly and under stress.
4. The capability to fire, reload and clear the weapon one handed, either hand.
5. Having equal skills in various firing positions including prone, kneeling and off-hand.
6. The ability to utilize cover either on the left or on the right.
7. Having equal skills at night.

All of these skills can be acquired by attending training classes or by simply practicing. There are so many DVDs, books and training classes out there for rifle skills I could not begin to list them all.

Developing advanced skills is not cheap and requires a lot of time. Since I consider shooting a recreational activity, it passes my "dual usage" rule.

The typical beginning carbine or rifle class will teach you the basics. These are normally 2-day affairs and cost between $800-$1500, not counting ammunition or travel. They are worth every penny for a beginner.

You can also arrange for private lessons and should inquire at your local gun store about instructors.

Once you master the basics, it is simply a matter of practice to get to an expert level.

Fighting skills with a rifle are perishable. Like any other eye-hand activity, it takes continual practice.

Some other ideas for gaining advanced skills would be Airsoft or paintball. There are leagues, competitions and numerous other organized events for both of these training tools. Airsoft rifles shoot plastic BBs that sting a little, but are not harmful. Even elite military units use them to train. You can have a full-fledged firefight, with realistic circumstances that is cheap and safe.

8.1.2 Long Range Marksman

I intentionally listed two categories concerning long range shooting, because being a sniper is a lot different from a long range marksman. While a sniper is a long range shooter, a long range shooter is NOT a sniper.

There is always a debate about the value of a long range shooter in a survival or defensive mode. One school of thought believes that the typical civilian marksman will not pull the trigger on a target at distance because of potential misidentification. This line of thinking believes hesitation and "what if" questions will delay the actual shot until it is too late.

The other side of this argument is that a sniper, through long range tactical influence, is the most potent weapon on the battlefield. The thinking is that a long range marksman will have the same impact during the defense of a location.

I personally fall into the second group. If things are really bad and you know anyone approaching is dangerous, then the capability to get to them before they can get to you is priceless. In addition, I have never seen a long range shooter who was not skilled at closer ranges, so even if the situation is difficult to call, the shooter can contribute at closer ranges.

I rate someone a Long Range Marksman if they can hit man-sized targets over 80% of the time at 600 meters and over 60% of the time at 900 meters.

While there are schools and training available to teach long range shooting, they are not as common as "normal" rifle classes. The best way to develop this skill is to learn about ballistics, bullet drop and hold over – AND THEN GO PRACTICE.

Don't be discouraged if your progress is a little slow. Shooting extreme distances takes skill, control and practice, practice, practice.

8.2 Special Skills

Not all activity involved in the defense of a location involves pulling a trigger. A modern military unit has 4-5 Logistic and Support personnel for every single trigger puller. Troops have to eat, receive medical care, be transported and all sorts of jobs that have nothing to do with actual fighting.

Since this is a book on defense, our primary focus is on that topic, but that is not to make light of support and logistics. They are critical as well.

When one thinks of a post-event world, medical care has to be a serious concern just in daily life, let alone if there is gunfire involved. A simple scratch could lead to infection, and without a supply of antibiotics, death.

There are several ways to increase your Group Rating in the Special Skills area. Most of them are interesting and educational and may have application in pre-event life. Here are a few suggestions:

1. Small engine repair. Given that generators could be the primary source of electrical power and most are driven by small engines, this could be a valuable skill.
2. EMT or advanced first aid training. There are normally community college courses available as well as free basic courses from the Red Cross and other agencies.
3. Small electronics repair should be in high demand in a post-event world. Radios, walkie-talkies, GPS units, computers, cameras and other devices used for security will eventually break.
4. Engineering of power systems, such as solar or generator driven will probably be needed. Any knowledge of irrigation, water supply and pumping could be invaluable.
5. Being a gunsmith may be extremely valuable in a post-event world. Basic skills like reloading ammunition would be useful as well.

All of these special skills would help with defense, and probably life in general in a post-event world.

9. Low Rise Apartments and Condos

Low Rise Apartment buildings are a bit of a quandary for preppers. While they have several positive aspects concerning defense, their typical shortfall is in the area of storage, as having enough food and water for a TEOTWAWKI existence takes up a lot of room.

This issue is not insurmountable by any means; it simply takes additional planning and resources.

A very clever idea for the renting prepper is the off-site storage facility. These are typically a locked, secure location rented on a month-to-month basis and normally full of odds and ends that cannot be stored in the primary domain. A prepper can keep food, water and other equipment relatively safe in one of these units and retrieve it later when necessary.

I recommend that the renting prepper also keep track of "empty" apartments close to their unit. In a complete break-down, these can become your own private warehouse if necessary. If the post-event world is hostile, you will not want to make a lot of trips to the storage facility.

The other major concern with most apartments is a single way in and out. This can become a "fatal funnel" if bad guys are trying to "storm the keep" and you want to get out. Even if you are not being attacked, you are easy to scout and a looter might just wait until you leave to try and restock his backpack, or just occupy your nicely prepared position and wait for you to come home.

If TEOTWAWKI has occurred, the apartment building manager is probably not going to be concerned if you were to "make a backdoor" into an adjoining unit or other area. While this would be considerable work, it could be a possibility for an emergency escape route. Be warned that some building codes require a "firewall" between apartment units or within sections of any multi-unit building, so you might be looking at a concrete wall. HVAC ducts might also be an option, but most of these are too small for a human to make it through. The Israeli Army actually started using a procedure similar to this some time ago. Sections of Palestine are densely populated with narrow streets and numerous places for "insurgents" to hide and attack Israeli patrols. The Israelis changed their procedures after years of causalities and now try and avoid the streets by "blasting" doorways through the interior of buildings. Holes punched through a wall here or there can make a "tunnel system" of sorts and allows their soldiers to "bypass" dangerous areas by staying away from exposed areas.

If you consider the "average" apartment complex layout, there are several positive attributes to defend such a location. The diagram that follows illustrates a "typical" layout, which from an overhead view, resembles a **fort**.

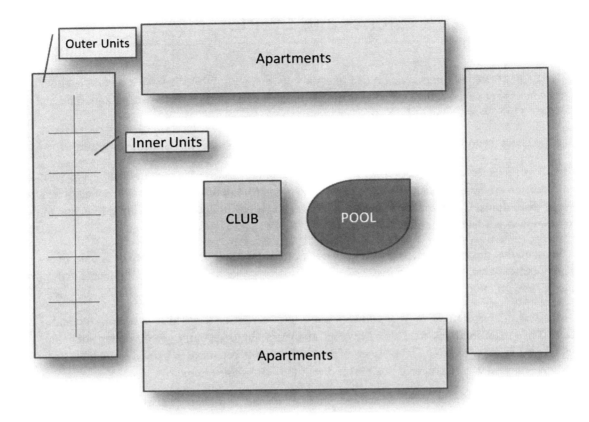

Figure 55 - Typical Apartment Complex Overview

You can see in Figure 55, a series of buildings surrounds a common area with a pool, clubhouse, gardens or other ammenities. Parking and nearby streets would normally be on the outside of the buildings.

Between each building, there is a walkway for tenants to access the inner units and common area. If you have one of the "inner" units, you do not have to be as diligent about visibility, light discipline and noise discipine as the typical home owner unless you are concerned about your neighbors.

Being a renting prepper has several advantages:

1. Normally with apartment complexes, the greater the population density, the more security features will be present. Fencing, steel doors, gated parking and other features designed to make the potential resident feel more secure are considered a competitive advantage.
2. A renter probably knows their neighbors as well as any single family neighborhood. While renters tend to be more "transient" than home owners, they typically choose a complex based on features attractive to their tastes and demographics. This means that they have a lot in common with their fellow tenants and relationships are established.
3. A renter can be selective on their next lease. Even if your current complex does not cater to a defensive position, when you shop for your next apartment you can make a selection with

defendability as a desirable criteria. A home owner has to either modify their location, or wait until they move, which is a more complex process for them.

EWS and ADS are practically unusable for the average Apartment complex unless all of the occupants organize and group together (highly unlikely). You cannot string EWS devices between the buildings unless all of the tennets know they are there. You could block these access areas with vehicles or post-event fencing, but you should make sure they are a true ADS. Evil looter types could simply hop over a couple of cars blocking the access route.

Another important item is door security, especially if there is only a single way in and out. While the typical apartment has steel or fireproof doors already installed, these are not a magic shields. You should prepare to heavily reinforce that door so as it takes an armored vehicle to knock it down.

I would also recommend you have extensive fire fighting capabilities. In a sense, being in an apartment can be compared to being in a cave or bunker. It won't take long for some frustrated attacker to decide to just smoke or burn you out if you are putting up a stiff resistence.

Here are some of my recommendations for renting preppers:

1. Establishing a group or team with your fellow tenants is critical for renters. If you can agree upon a pact with a few others that an "attack on one is an attack on all", then anyone trying to breach your unit would have to worry about who is behind them. This allows for multiple angles of fire as described in Section 6.11.
2. Choose an "inner" unit if at all possible. As stated, the advantages of visibility, light and noise discipline are worth the lack of view.
3. When considering a new lease, view potential sites with an eye towards security. How would I loot this complex? How easy would it be to get in and get out? What is the surrounding neighborhood like? Most renters look for secuirty features anyway, so this should not be an entirely new way of thinking.
4. Choose a second or third story unit if you can manage the stairs on a daily basis. As stated in previous sections, holding the high ground has several advantages. You may also be able to implement ADS or EWS on the stairs leading to your abode.

10. Highrise Apartments and Condos

Author's note: of all of the "common" housing types available, highrise living presents more potential issues with Defense than any other. I personally have lived in two different apartment buildings (23rd and 44th floors) and while that lifestyle has its advantages, I felt like I would be in a bad position if it "all went to hell." If you live in a highrise, I recommend that you have an alternate bug out location. Plan for occupying an abondanded commercial building close by, store a camper or bug out to relatives. If there are not any alternative solutions available to you, the following section may help and I sincerely wish you well.

At first glance, a highrise building appears to be an extremely secure location and one of the easiest to defend. Taller buildings are normally constructed of steel reinforced concrete and this can be a very secure environment. A major issue with any apartment is storage, as stocking enough food and water for a TEOTWAWKI existence takes up a lot of space.

The storage issue is not insurmountable by any means; it simply takes additional planning and resources.

As stated before, a good idea for the renting prepper is the off-site storage facility. These are typically a locked, secure location that is rented on a month-to-month basis and normally full of odds and ends that cannot be stored in the primary domain. A prepper can keep their food, water and other equipment relatively safe in one of these units and retrieve it later when necessary.

The renting prepper should keep track of "empty" apartments close by their unit. In a complete break-down, these can become your own private warehouse if necessary. If the post-event world is hostile, you will want to make a lot of trips to the storage facility.

Another concept for the "home in the sky" prepper is a mini-van or similar vehicle accessible in the building's parking garage. You could conceivably store your food and water offsite, retrieve it when the time is right and hide it in the garage with a careful disguise.

My single biggest concern about skyscraper living in a post-event world is **fire**. Even if the starving masses are not looting and burning, electrical power and water pressure may not exist. You have several options for drinking water, but a fire started on a lower floor by any means would be a very big problem. While fire protection for your floor or specific unit may not be an unsolvable problem, extinguishing a building wide blaze would be practically impossible.

If there is no electrical power, the elevators are not going to work. This is both a positive and a negative since any potential scallywags would have to climb the stairs – but so will you. It might be possible to rig a rope and hoist heavy loads up to your floor rather than you hauling everything up the stairs.

If you have to fallback, your escape routes are very limited. A rope ladder over a balcony might work if you are not on a higher floor.

Taller buildings are often attractive to tenants for "the view." This, again, has advantages and disadvantages from a defensive standpoint. While it would have a very good observation point and over watch position, it has a Visibility Factor from a considerable distance, so your light and noise discipline would have to be very well executed.

If you have an apartment or condo on a higher floor, I recommend you plan your defenses for the entire floor, not just your specific unit. Stairwells, fire escapes and other access points would be prime candidates for EWS devices to let you know if someone is entering your immediate area. Establishment of a group or team would likely be more realistic with the people on the same floor rather than the entire building. Tennant association meetings, the building's gym and recreation facilities might be good places to scout for potential co-preppers.

An ADS is possible on higher units, but be aware of cutting off escape routes for fire or egress. Stairwell doors (normally steel) can be welded or sealed in some way without much effort. You need to make sure that you, or any people above you, will never have to exit that way in a hurry.

Taller buildings have a flat roof, and there are urban survival guides that suggest you could grow food and defend from that position. I would warn about the wisdom of defending from a rooftop for a couple of reasons:

1. If your building is not the tallest around, you risk being scouted and approached later. Roof top movements or activity would be EASY to spot even from lower positions.
2. Shooting from a steep angle is not the same as regular marksmanship. I don't know of very many places to practice shooting from 20+ stories above the target that won't receive a hasty visit from the local SWAT team. *While Charles Whitman, who in 1964 started shooting from the 27th floor of the* Texas Tower *in Austin, did kill 14 people, he was a trained United States Marine with a Sharpshooter's badge. It should be noted that his ADS was completely ineffective, or the carnage would have been even more horrific. The police simply kicked his door jamb out of the way and took care of business.*

11. Weapons

If you are a gun person, feel free to skip this chapter. It is written for those who have little experience with firearms.

Weapons (guns) are like automobiles or practically anything else – they are a compromise. In the case of weapons, the compromises are between weight, power, reliability, cost, availability of ammo and all sorts of other factors.

Any rifle is a machine, and like all machines, they can break or fail. There are a couple of "old sayings" that seriously apply to weapons:

"Buy nice or buy twice" is really true. For the most part, you get what you pay for in a weapon. There are too many manufactures out there in competition for everyone's money. Will a $1,000 rifle shoot better or last longer than a $2,000 dollar rifle of a similar platform – not likely. This rule holds true until you start getting into the exotic big game or hunting rifles. Some of these "works of art" go for tens of thousands of dollars and are worth it to their specialized market. I would not invest in one of these types of rifles for a defense weapon, long range or medium range.

"One is none – Two is one" is another old adage that really rings true. Even the highest quality, well maintained weapons can jam or break. What is intended by this wisdom is that you need a backup weapon. Most professional soldiers refer to it as a "secondary", and that is normally a pistol. I apply the 1=0, 2=1 rule differently as a prepper in that I am not sure my local gunsmith will be around to fix my broken weapons, so I have two of all of my weapons for spare parts.

For our Security Planning, you need to categorize weapons into three primary functions:

- Long Range
- Medium Range
- Close Quarters Combat

Figure 56 - AR15 Mocking How Many Accessories Some People Mount on Their Rifles

Long range weapons are types and calibers of rifles that have an extended range. For our purposes, I will define Long Range as over 500 yards (450 meters).

One of the first decisions you have to make regarding long range weapons is what a realistic upper range limit is. Set your expectations at a reasonable level. Despite what you may see on TV, or read in books, hitting a man sized target at over 600 meters is **NOT** easy. While any accomplished hunter or long range shooter can probably handle that shot a majority of the time, the average person who only occasionally shoots will have a low hit rate. I have met guys who purchase a .50 BMG rifle (about the biggest caliber you can buy) because they want to hit targets at 1500 yards or more. Many of these weapons become "gun safe queens" because it is VERY difficult to find somewhere to even practice at that range, let alone make a very complex shot.

The range you need for this type of weapon will also depend on the terrain around your location. If you will be in a desert, then long range shots are more realistic. If you will be in an urban or heavily wooded area, then you may not have a "line of sight" over 600 yards.

Another factor is target identification. Can you really discern between friend and foe at over 1,000 yards? Do you have the optics (binoculars or spotting scope) to tell the difference between a bad guy carrying an AK47 and a neighbor carrying a shovel at great distance? Even if you could, would you want to take a risky shot at that distance and give away your position?

My final factor for the analysis of long range hardware is stopping power. Any medium to large caliber is going to deliver a serious injury to a human, but there is also the stopping power for vehicles to consider. One of my personal nightmares concerns the accessibility of my location by vehicle. You could literally DRIVE right up to the front door. Now before you go thinking I am being a little paranoid here, think about the news footage of every conflict in the last 40 years. What do you commonly see? The military refers to them as a "technical" or civilian cars or trucks that have been modified to fight.

Figure 57 - Example of a "Technical" Modified Fighting Vehicle

Every "resource challenged" gang of fighters in the world seems to eventually figure out that you can mount a machine gun on the back of a pickup truck, line the bed with sandbags and have a very potent platform from which to project power. In the event of an extended gunfight at your location, how long would it be before some desperate fellow decides to drive the truck right through your front door? Could your large caliber weapon stop it?

Really, any quality hunting rifle will do, but there are a few considerations you should take into account:

1. Availability of ammunition is a key factor. For over 40 years, the military's primary sniper rifle has been a .308 Winchester caliber. The .308 is extremely popular with police and law enforcement departments and hunters as well. Of all of the long range calibers, I would estimate that there is more .308 out there than any other caliber. (In the last five years, larger caliber sniper rifles have come into favor with the military, including the .50 BMG and the .338 LM.)

2. Cost of ammunition is another key factor for most of us. We want to practice with our rifle, especially a long range weapon. So the cost of your ammunition inventory as well as practice ammo is a serious consideration.

3. As a rule, for a long range weapon, the optics (scope) should cost about as much as the actual weapon.

Model	Caliber	Description	Price
Remington 700	Several	Very common bolt-action rifle. Several models available. Typically very accurate for the cost. Military uses them.	$600 - $6,000
LWRC REPR	.308	AR10 Style Auto-loader. Very accurate and reliable. Piston gun.	$2400- $2800
POF PX308	.308	AR10 Style Auto-loader. Very accurate and reliable. Piston gun.	$2400- $2800
Barrett	.50BMG & .338LM	Big, heavy, accurate. Long range (over a mile) capable. Military uses them.	$3500 - $10,000
FN SCAR	.308	Next Generation .308 battle rifles. Light, accurate.	$2500 - $2800

This list could go on and on. There are hundreds of weapons that would fit into this category. My intent was to list just a few samples. My personal long range weapon is a POF .308 with a 16 inch barrel. It is death incarnate at 900 meters and it will stop almost any non-armored vehicle within 200 meters.

In my humble opinion, there is no better medium range weapon for defense than an AR15 rifle. Here are my reasons:

1. Good balance of power: It was designed to take down a man out to 400 meters yet has very little recoil. Most women shoot it comfortably. It will leave enough of a rabbit to eat, yet can take down a large deer.

2. Easy to use: The weapon was designed for high school age draftees to use in battle. The controls are simple and the weapon is easy to maintain.

3. Reasonable initial cost: As of this writing, a reasonable quality AR15 can be purchased at around $950.00. Purchase an "Optics Ready Carbine" and a cheap Red Dot optic (less than $50.00) and you are good-to-go.

4. Availability of Ammo: The AR15 shoots a military round (5.56 NATO) or in civilian terms, .223 caliber (*there are some minor differences, but almost all modern AR15 rifles will shoot both*). This is one of the most common rounds out there and good quality ammo abounds. A box of 20 plinking rounds can be purchased for $6.00. Good quality fighting ammo runs $10-15 per 20 rounds. There are some 'experts' who believe that if the world goes to hell in a hand basket, AR15 ammo will be more valuable than gold or bread.

5. Availability of Parts: Since it is a military grade weapon, parts are easy to get in almost any town that has a gun store. Any Army rifle uses all the same parts as well.

6. Flexibility: There is no other single weapon on the planet that has more options than an AR15. It is kind of like the Harley Davidson of guns – you can customize it to practically any configuration. Flashlights, lasers, different stocks, sights, night vision, rails, slings – you name it gun-wise, you can do it to an AR15.

7. Reliability: It is a military grade weapon. You can drop it, submerge it, bury it, coat it in sand and completely abuse the weapon and it will still go boom when you pull the trigger. If you are not a gun person then the bug out weapon will probably end up in the closet getting dusty. An AR15 will not rust and dust won't bother it at all.

8. Investment: AR15s hold their value. If you purchase one, and decide later it is unnecessary, you can typically get close to your purchase price back at any gun show.

BUT THE MOST IMPORTANT FACTOR!

IT LOOKS EVIL

There is zero doubt about what it is and sometimes, **intimidation** is enough. If you are holding grandpa's duck gun when I come to steal the gas out of your bug out buggy, I know for a fact it holds less than 8 rounds and you can go screw yourself outside of 75 yards. If you are holding an AR15, I am thinking there might be a better target for my ill intent. I cannot stress enough to become familiar with your weapon of choice for home defense or as bug out weapon. Know how it works, how to clean it and practice with it. In a confrontation, it is difficult enough when you are a highly trained, experienced operator. For 99.999 percent, the confrontation is never going to happen – but in a bug out situation, where you are probably stressed beyond belief already, it is nice to know you can take care of the worst case scenario. A good weapon, with a little practice, will provide that piece of mind.

In reality, any military grade weapon would be a good choice. A lot of knowledgeable people like AK47s and SKS Assault Rifles. FALs, Mini-14s and other types of multiple shot "fighting" rifles are also popular. The table below lists some options and general pricing.

Model	Description	Price
POF (Various)	AR15 Piston Guns – Very highly rated	$1700 - $2400
Smith & Wesson M&P 15	Fair quality, standard parts	$950-$1100
LWRC (Various)	AR15 Piston Guns – Very highly rated	$1700 - $2400
Colt (Various)	AR15 GI guns, built to military specs	$1400 - $2000
Bravo Company USA	AR15 GI funs, built to military specs	$1100 - $1400
Bushmaster ACR	Next generation combat weapon, uses AR15 magazines	$2200 - $2400

AK47 (Any make)	Most popular assault weapon in the world	$650 - $900
SKS (Any make)	Eastern Block assault weapon, surpluses to US in great quantities	$350 - $500
FAL (Any make)	British Assault rifle used by both sides in Falkland's War – .308 – heavy, but popular	$900 - $2200

There are over 30 manufactures of AR15 platform weapons as of this writing. If you count the other types of rifles, the number probably gets into the hundreds.

For Close Quarters Combat, we are talking about either a pistol or a shotgun. Again, despite what you see on TV, outside of 75 yards, a shotgun is not effective[12]. Outside of 50 yards, even the best pistol is marginal. In reality, the combat ranges are really more likely 50 and 20 yards respectively.

What shotguns and pistols excel at is close quarters fighting. If attackers make it within your location (home), a rifle is heavy, long and unwieldy for going around corners or fast maneuvers around furniture. Any pistol caliber 9mm or above (.40, 10mm, .45, .38, .44mag) will do the job. My personal preference is a .45 for a variety of reasons, but I know a lot of VERY accomplished "door kickers" who use a 9mm. I am not even going to try and list pistol options. There are hundreds of models from dozens of manufactures available. A good gun store can let you hold and feel several models to see what is best for your hand and eye.

For a shotgun, a 12 gauge is really the only option worth considering. Shotguns come in a variety of different configurations, but for a defensive weapon, there are two basic options: A pump or an Autoloader. Get the shortest barrel, highest capacity model you can afford. For shotguns, autoloaders tend to be about twice as expensive as pumps. I have seen experts who can fire a pump as fast as any autoloader, but they have practiced this for years. Some example models and estimated prices are:

Model	Description	Price
Remington 870	Pump – Specialized Defense models available	$350-$600
Benelli M4	Automatic – Used by the US Marines, **best of the best**	$1700 - $1850
Mossberg 530	Pump – Specialized Defense models available	$400-$600
Mossberg 930 SPX	Automatic – Used by several Police departments	$600-$700

Again, these are just a few samples of the hundreds of various shotgun makes/models available.

Pistols come in two basic flavors – revolvers and automatics. The term automatic is a bit misleading as it is not a full automatic weapon, but rather one pull of the trigger fires one round. Revolvers are simpler,

---

[12] Some specialized military rounds have extended range, but these are rare.

more reliable and often less expensive. They are slow to reload (unless you are an expert) and do not hold as many rounds. Automatics are more complex to operate, but hold more rounds, are faster to reload and are typically a little more accurate under combat stress due to the lighter trigger pull.

I am not even going to attempt a table on pistols as there are SO MANY OPTIONS. Look for a local shooting range that offers rentals. They typically will have most popular models for you to rent and see how they fit your hand/eye.

My personal pistols are all 1911 style .45 ACP. You can get a fair quality 1911 for less than $500, and can pay upwards of $3800 for a custom, competition grade weapon of the same model. Glocks are very popular pistols as well and some professionals swear by them.

Asking someone what the "best" weapon is, is like asking someone "what is the best movie ever made." What kind of movie? What era? What mood am I in? You can tell someone what YOUR favorite is, but debates will rage for hours over which one is/was BEST.

11.1 Optics

There has been more development in firearm's optics (tools to aim the weapon) in the last 15 years than any other category. With the onset of lasers, red dots, holographic gun sights and scope technologies, the tools that can be used for the modern day shooter are far more capable than just a few years prior. Like any topic, there are a few key terms that will help you understand this world and make solid decisions as you equip for your defense.

BUIS (Back Up Iron Sights) are the original[13] post and fork that we all grew up with as kids on our BB guns. For over 300 years, iron sights were state of the art. Now, you will notice, they have the name "back up". This is because the newer technologies have been proven to be faster on target and more accurate under pressure.

A **Red Dot** optic is a laser beam that is projected onto a small, clear glass mounted on the weapon. Red Dot's should not be confused with Holographic sights, nor should they be compared with aiming lasers. When you look through the sight, you simply put the "dot" on the target and squeeze the trigger. Red Dot sights are typically inexpensive, with some bargain models going for $30 or less. Be careful, because most of the inexpensive models are not water or fog proof and the battery life tends to be very short.

---

[13] Professionals don't trust optics much. Batteries can fail; glass gets shattered and other battlefield injuries can occur. A real pro learns to use their BUIS first and well and this is good advice for the Prepper as well.

Most SERIOUS shooters or professionals choose a Holographic Sight, which is the same basic principle, but normally is more robust, has a longer battery life and the most important of all – much less parallax. You will notice in the last picture that the "dot" is off to the side, or off center of the glass. This is called parallax and can cause a missed shot. Holographic sites eliminate a large amount of parallax.

Holographic Weapons Sights are similar to Red Dots, but the image seen when looking through them is generated by a holographic device rather than a straight laser beam.

The image on the left shows a typical Holographic image looking through the optic. The soldier on the right (showing very bad shooting form) is looking through a Trijicon ACOG optic.

Trijicon Inc. is a company that makes a type of optic called an ACOG (Advanced Combat Optic Gunsight), which is favored by military professionals all over the world. The ACOG is a unique combination of magnification, red dot and is self-illuminating (requires no batteries). An ACOG is expensive, but the quality and reliability are famous throughout the services. The fact that it never needs a battery should perk the attention of most preppers. *I own several of them.*

Several non-gun people have asked me "why don't soldiers use the most magnification possible? Wouldn't it be better to always zoom in as close as possible?"

The answer to this is no, it is not better and the reason why is target acquisition and the speed of acquisition. A very high magnification rifle scope makes it difficult to find a target close to you, and the typical gun fight is within 200 meters.

For sniping, a high magnification scope is a great help and is commonly used, but for targets inside of 200 meters, it is the speed you can acquire and fire that counts.

Rifle scopes come in about as many varieties as actual rifles and pistols. Again, buy nice or buy twice. I think every gun guy in the world has pondered if the higher priced optics are "worth it", especially when the stores are full of much lower cost units. My personal experience is that any rifle scope that costs less than $500 is suspect. Any rifle scope that costs above $3,000 is suspect. The differences between lower cost scopes and the higher priced models are:

> **Light Transmission** – A good quality scope will allow you to see better as light fades.

> **Hold of Zero** – Poor quality scopes will not hold the crosshairs at zero while mounted on a rifle with heavier recoil. You shoot the rifle a few times and start noticing that you are missing your target all-of-sudden.

> **Quality of housing** – A good quality scope can be used as a hammer to drive a nail. While this may sound a little silly, if you ever drop your rifle down the side of a cliff and find that the scope is still intact and holds zero, you will think your investment was wise.

> **Adjustments** – A higher quality scope will have more finite adjustments.

> *A VERY important note to make about any optic or scope that is intended for a fighting gun – don't skimp on the mounting system! A fighting weapon will take more abuse than any hunting weapon and requires a quality, proven mounting system.*

I am also going to include **Aiming Lasers** under the topic of Optics, although technically, they are not a true "optic."

An aiming laser puts a small dot on the target. You pull the trigger when the dot is where you want the bullet to go.

You can purchase aiming lasers for rifles and for most pistols. I am not a big fan of aiming lasers on rifles because they give away your position. On the other hand, I think they have a place on a handgun, since my target will already know where I am if I am using a handgun anyway. You may decide differently.

11.2 Accessories

Accessories (sometimes referred to as furniture) are all of the nice little items you attach or use with your weapon. A sling is an example of an accessory. Accessories are typically a matter of personal preference and thousands of choices are available. Some of the most common accessories are:

- Slings
- Weapon Lights
- Rails
- Stocks
- Lasers
- Pods
- Bi-Pods
- Multi-magazine devices

Of all of the Accessories, I believe a **sling** is the most important for a defensive weapon. A good, comfortable sling is critical because you will hopefully be carrying the weapon more than shooting it. Slings are categorized by how many points they attach to the weapon with. Single point, two point and three point slings are the only ones I know of. By far, the most popular is the two point sling.

When you are trying on a sling, make sure you can transition the weapon around to your back. If you are out working the garden, but feel the need for security, then you are not going to want to hang onto the gun with one hand or have it swinging around your waist and knees. *My personal favorite is the Magpul MS2.*

11.2.1   For Reference

There are some companies whose equipment you just can't go wrong with. I have compiled a list below for your reference and I am sure that I will leave some very good products/companies off of the list by accident. These are firms I have done business with and have had great results.

Company	General Category
LWRC	Rifles
Springfield Armory	Pistols (I am not a fan of their rifles)
POF	Rifles
Bravo Company USA	Rifles and Accessories
LMT	Rifles

Trijicon	Optics and ACOGs – Anything with the Trij name is quality
Zeiss	Optics – make sure you get the German made
Schmidt and Bender	Optics (very high end)
Leupold	Mid-range optics
LaRue	Accessories and Rifles – anything with the Larue name on it is top quality
Magpul	Accessories – anything from Magpul is top of the line
Elcan	Optics (very high end)
Surefire	Lights and other weapons accessories (very high end)

If you don't find the name of the product you are looking at on this list, don't consider that as a negative. If you do see the name on this list, you can count on a good value for your money at worst. I have purchased many products from these firms with positive results and excellent customer service.

Note: air rifles and bows are common items with many preppers. They make sense to hunt without the typical noise signature of a powder based gun. I have not included them here because as defensive weapons, they are limited in range and air rifles are not as "silent" as you might imagine.

11.3 Other Equipment

11.3.1   Night Vision

There is lots of equipment you can purchase to improve your defensive capabilities. Probably the biggest "game changer" I have ever spent money on is night vision.

A Night Vision Device or NVD is rated in "Generations", with Gen1, 2, 3 or 4 being currently available. The price goes up as the generation does. For our purposes, a Generation 3 device is all that we need.

In addition to the generation of the device, you also need to verify that it is "gated", which means it can withstand bright lights, like the muzzle flash of a weapon, without damage.

NVD comes is several different configurations. You can purchase dedicated weapons sights, goggles and monocles. I have found that the monocles are the most useful in that you can mount them on an AR15 in front of your normal optics (if you purchase the right kind of optics), as well as use them stand-alone.

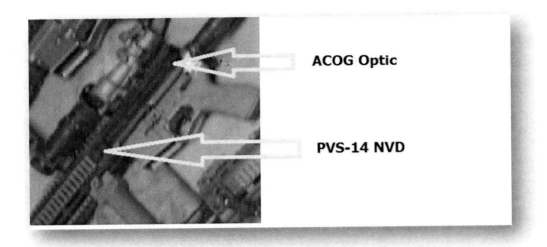

Figure 58 - Author's Rifle with NVD Mounted in Front of ACOG

A Generation 3 NVD is so effective you can drive, safely, at night without headlights. I can also hunt effectively at night and that could be important in a post-event environment. NVD **will not** see through smoke or fog. You need Infrared for that capability.

Unless your foe has NVD, you will own the night. On average, one third of our time on this earth is in low or no light conditions.

As of this writing, a quality Gen-3 monocles, such as a PVS-14, is about $2900. That is a lot of cash, but again, I can't think of a single item you can purchase for the same money that will improve your capabilities as much as NVD.

In the last few years, Forward Looking Infrared (FLIR) devices have become available to the general public. These units are extremely expensive, ranging from $6,000 to over $25,000. FLIR devices give the added advantage of being able to see through smoke and some amounts of fog. Personally, I can't justify the expense for my intended purposes. I also keep an eye on the prices as they continue to decline. When FLIR technology approaches the price of existing Light Gathering NVD, then I will probably consider a purchase, but not before then.

NOTE: NVDs are battery powered. Most take standard sizes, such as AA, so a rechargeable is a valid option.

11.3.2   Body Armor

Body armor is rated in "levels", such as Level -3 or Level- 4. Level- 3 armor is rated to stop all handgun rounds and most rifle rounds fired from a distance. The rating system on body armor is very complex because it has to be able to withstand multiple hits in a wide variety of temperatures. For our purposes, we probably won't be fighting in arctic conditions.

Level- 4 armor is basically for the military and the situations they are exposed to. While you may end up in a gun fight, chances are you will not end up being shelled or expect your armor to withstand the effects of missile strikes.

I have a Level 3 soft sided vest I purchased for $460.00 new. It weighs just a bit over 3 pounds. I think it is worth every penny.

11.3.3   Accessories

Figure 59 - Practice Day for the Author

I use **knee pads**. If you ever practice going prone quickly, you may wish you had them. I also recommend a good pair of **shooting gloves**. Gun barrels get very hot and there are always splinters, sharp edges and lots of glass around when people are shooting at each other.

I also believe strongly in **ear protection**. You can purchase in-the-ear models that let regular sound through (like talking or shouted communication) but block the majority of rifle discharge. As we stated above, shooting in an enclosed area, like a home, can permanently damage your hearing. This, combined with the fact that we need to communicate with each other during this time makes ear protection very important. Be aware of battery requirements.

I cannot stress enough to have **eye protection**. I am not worried about my gun exploding in my face or anything like that – my concern is if someone is shooting at me, there is going to be sand, glass, plaster, stone and just about anything else flying through the air around me. I use a good pair of wrap-around glasses. The Army issues goggles, but I have always had fogging issues with tight sealing goggles. I have to wear prescription glasses to read, so eye protection takes on a whole new level of investment.

I use a **chest-rig**, or **load vest**. This is a device that you strap on and attach various "pouches" to via a system called MOLLE (Pronounced Molly), or Modular Lightweight Load-Carrying Equipment. MOLLE rigs, pouches and accessories are available in many configurations. An Army Surplus Store or your local well-stocked gun shop is a great place to start looking. MOLLE equipment allows you to carry all sorts of things around your chest and mid-section while keeping your hands free to do other things. You want some of this stuff, such as spare magazines, available to you without taking off a backpack. MOLLE rigs are not expensive. You can get an average setup for less than $50.00.

I keep a basic kit on my chest-rig to **maintain** my weapons. This is a little more than just a gun cleaning kit. It contains, for example, a simple flat bladed screw driver because on the rare case when an AR15 does jam up tight, I have the best chance to get it back in action with a screw driver. The average military grade weapon can go thousands of rounds without requiring a cleaning. Most of them, including the AR15, run better when kept "wet" or lubed. As you practice with your defensive weapons, you will figure out what goes wrong with them. I always recommend people purchase some of the cheapest, most likely to jam ammunition they can find to familiarize themselves with what can go wrong with the weapon and how to clear it and get it back in action.

Most people do not put much faith in their **cell phones** in a post-event world, and this could be a mistake. While cell towers most likely will not be available for calls, if your phone has a built-in GPS (Global Positioning System), then it can be a great tool for defense. A phone with a GPS receiver will work off satellites (if they are gone we are all in trouble) and still function. In addition, there are applications you can download to modern "smart phones" that use the GPS receiver in all kinds of interesting ways. For example, you can set a location on the phone and then the phone will take you back to it later. This is advertised as being able to help you find your car in a busy parking lot, but we can use it for Rally Points or other functions where we need to meet or you have hidden supplies. Another application, commonly referred to as a Cell Phone Tracker, or Cell Phone Locator , can show you on a map where other members of your party are located. Be careful when selecting one of the applications that does not require the network, but simply work off of the transmitter within the phone. This is an amazing technology that the U.S. Army has spent millions of dollars to develop (more capable version). It allows you to see where each of your defenders are on a map if they are within range of your transmitter (about 1 mile depending on terrain) and that could be critical in the field.

Anyone who likes to watch action movies has probably seen the depiction of a "silencer" being used on a weapon. The weapon, when fired, makes a sound similar to my mother-in-law's reaction to her Christmas presents – *pfffffsssst*. In the real world, silencers don't exist as depicted. There are however, noise reduction devices call **Suppressors** (or a **CAN**) that you can put on a weapon with the proper "tax stamp" from the government (ATF). While these devices do not "silence" the weapon, they do reduce the noise significantly and in a post-event world, this could be a big advantage. Imagine being able to fire at attackers, long range, and they can't determine where the shot came from. You could also hunt without giving away your location on every shot. Your local gun shop can give you the legal requirements and availability for your area. *Please note – most suppressors require a specific threading or type of barrel to attach to your weapon, so make sure you verify everything will fit when considering this option.*

12. The Rules of Engagement

Most of us have heard the term "Rules of Engagement." This is normally an official, written order issued by Military Commands, to assure compliance with political policy. In laymen's terms, it is "Who can we shoot, under what circumstances."

For those who prepare, the Rules of Engagement take on a little different meaning, because in a post-event world, they will probably change often.

It is impossible for this book, or any other source to recommend Rules of Engagement for location defense, because the scenario has NEVER occurred before.

What is important is that some sort of rules be established as part of your plan. They can range from "I am the leader, and I will make the call every single time", to a lengthy list of options and actions.

The leader may not always be available (off site scavenging), so some sort of basic "policy" should be established as part of your defensive plan. On the opposite side, a complex set of instructions will be difficult to follow under stress.

Only you know your group, their mindset and their capabilities. There are, however, several considerations that will most likely come into play:

- Is everyone approaching your location a threat?
- Is everyone approaching your location bait, or a trap?
- Will your group barter?
- Do you honor a white flag?
- Will your group accept new members post event?

The list of questions and scenarios is practically endless.

At minimum, your "Rules of Engagement" should include:

- The position everyone should take when contact is made or approaching people are detected.
- The action everyone should take if fired upon.

Knowing the position everyone should take is an interesting example. In an active defense, you may want some of your shooters in plain sight. In a passive defense, you don't want anyone visible.

What if the contact is just a scouting mission and your location is just being sized up?

There are also some simple rules that everyone should know and agree to:

- You can take any action necessary to defend yourself.
- You can take any action necessary to defend the location and members of the group.

The Rules should be known and agreed upon by all members of the group. You don't want one of your aggressive members starting a firefight with some people who just want to barter.

In Chapter 4, The Event Horizon, we discussed how people will react over a period of time after an event. Your rules of engagement will probably become more harsh, or aggressive, as time moves from the Social Grace Period through the Desperation Period and then become more "friendly" as reorganization sets in.

Chapter 7 covered the definition of perimeters and zones. The distance away from your location should have an impact on your rules as well. One of the reasons why everyone in your group should know your perimeter definition is to be able to communicate and take action based on which zone the contact is in.

Another controversial topic is warning shots. I have never liked the concept of a warning shot, but have to admit it does have its positive attributes. A warning shot fired over someone's head can have several different results. It gives away at least one of your positions. It can also stop an innocent encounter without someone being hurt. It would be possible to debate various scenarios for hours and never reach a conclusion on the subject. You should probably have this debate with your group before trouble begins.

13. The Author's Plan

My family of four lives in a suburban area of a major metropolitan area. There is my lovely wife, a teenage son, daughter and myself. We have limited family in our area, which is my brother-in-law and his similar family of four (youngest being five years old). They live within walking distance. Our neighborhood, in the event of a total breakdown, is simply not defendable. The population density, ease of access, visibility ratings and other factors would make it difficult to hold. Aside from defensive issues with the location, there is not enough yard space for a garden, and the population density eliminates hunting.

My neighbor is a dear friend and fellow prepper. He is divorced, so the status of his sons being in our group is unknown. He owns a ranch about 1.5 hours away, and we have an open invitation to join him there should it "all go to Hell." He is an experienced hunter, has more weapons than I do (that is saying something), and has been in a gunfight. He is that rare "I got your back" type of man.

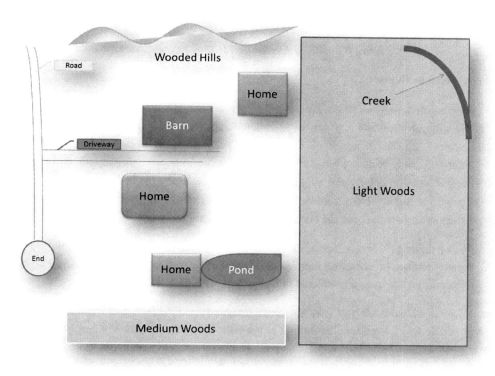

Figure 60 - The Ranch is the Author's BOL

The Ranch (Figure 60) is well wooded with three homes, a stocked lake and good game. It is well off of the beaten path. It is practically a prepper's paradise.

Our initial evaluation shows that even with our group of nine, we are short on defensive capabilities for a property of this size (100 Acres of Location Area).

Location Defense Worksheet

Location Factors	
Population Density	50
Proximity	1
Physical Area	448,000
Visibility	200
High Ground	2
Positions	3
Open Access	0
Limited Access	4
No Access	0
Location Rating	**37.54**

Figure 61 - Initial Evaluation Rating of the Ranch

I arrived at our rating as follows:

- The population density is 50 per square mile for that area.
- There is a major interstate highway at 11 miles, so the Proximity factor is 1.
- The Physical Area is 100 acres.
- The location is only visible from 1 road, 1 direction for 200 yards, thus the factor of 200.
- Most of the location is between hills, so the High Ground factor is low.
- There are three homes that would be occupied, so our initial positions are 3.
- Open Access and No Access are both zero. Access is limited from all directions.

I then carefully considered each member of my family, my brother-in-law's family and finally my neighbor. Since my brother-in-law has a smaller child, we have one dependent. Everyone else in our group is able bodied, but we have a couple of non-shooters with us.

My brother-in-law is a Mixed Martial Arts guy and I believe he would fight like a rabid dog. My son is very good with a rifle and I would welcome him at my side if trouble started. My neighbor, of course, has my back. We also have the benefit of a nurse as well as an engineer. My neighbor is an old farm boy, and is pretty handy, so he also added bonus points. There is a circle of friends that may or may not be able to get to the ranch. This is a hole in our plan as my neighbor and I have never talked about inclusion in our group other than family, so I have hardly discussed the location with anyone. Put that one on the "to do" list!

Group Factors	
Number of Defenders	8
No Firearms Experience	1
Basic Pistol Experience	1
Basic Rifle Experience	3
Advanced Firearms Experience	2
Long Range Marksman	1
Combat Vet	0
Trained Sniper	0
Condition of Group	
Restricted Mobility	0
Mobile	3
Physically Fit	3
Athletic	2
Number of Dependents	1
Special Skills	
Basic Medical (First Aid)	0
Medical (RN, EMT)	1
Doctor	0
Hunter	1
Engineer	1
Electronics	0
Machinist, Welder, Handyman	1
Mindset	
Timid or Unknown	1
Average	3
Aggressive	2
Has your back	1
Group Rating	23.50

Figure 62 - Group Rating for the Author's Plan

As you can see from Figures 61 and 62, we started off short on defensive capabilities.

The ranch is a big piece of property to count as a Location Area with this size group. Gathering food is going to be an issue, so we included all of it, because it will be a common activity being performed by everyone. We would stock up more than what we have, but by the time we transport our 15-day food supply, all the weapons ammo and gear, we can't carry any more in the bug-out-buggy (pickup truck). Making two trips might be an option, but after Hurricane Rita, just making a single trip concerns me. This means that we are going to need to garden, fish, and hunt while gathering food from the surrounding woods. The decision was made to hold and defend a 100 acre area.

The first item of business was to determine whether we are going with an active or passive initial posture. We decided on passive because the area is so remote, there is really no one around to get "active" for.

Many of the surrounding properties are "weekend" places, so it would not be unusual for the ranch to be unoccupied.

The next order of business was to reduce our Visibility Factor if necessary. Again, because of the remote location, combined with its being surrounded by wooded acreage, there really was not much to do here. The one thought that occurred to us was the road. The road leading up to the location is a single lane, gravel road that is really more of a lane than a road. We decided we would put up a façade that the road was "blocked" by a large tree branch. There was an area where this could be faked. We could even install a hidden, manual block and tackle system so we can remove the branch in short order if we wanted to get out.

This actually was a triple positive because it accomplished ADS and EWS all at the same time. The branch would be rigged with a tripwire and alarm in case someone tried to move the branch on their own, thus EWS.

The ADS was achieved because the roadway was taken away from any potential trouble makers. We also planned some "Road Closed" signs further away from the property.

Since there are three homes on the ranch, our number of positions and angles seemed good, but the layout did not allow for as much support as I would like. The barn was a fourth possibility, but it does not have any windows nor could I figure out any good fighting positions. It is actually a problem because it blocks any support from one of the homes (Old House in Figure 63).

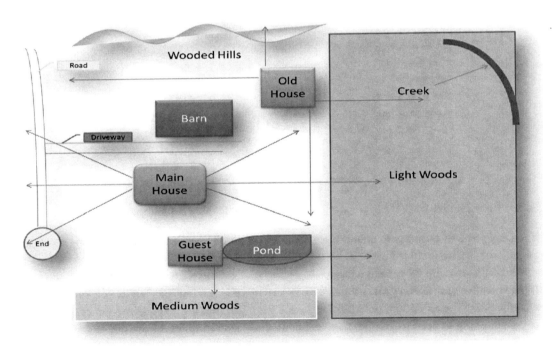

Figure 63 - Overview of the Ranch with Multiple Angles Shown by Arrows

We have six shooters in our group. The layout caused an issue because with a QRF, we were going to be short one position in one house (Guest House in Figure 63) and thus have a big blind spot. We considered placing the QRF person between the guest house and the main house in an exterior position, but that would hamper them from reinforcing the old house because they would have to cross in front of the defenders in the main house. Looked like a good way to get shot to me.

This simple, seemingly small point caused more discussion and stick drawings than any other part of the plan. I walked that ground at least a dozen times trying to work out the right way to do it. There just had to be a way, but everything we talked about was eliminated by some physical characteristic of the location.

In the end, we finally decided on a different solution – we need an additional shooter. As of this writing, that position has not been filled, but we are working on it.

We also decided that EWS were going to be a focus of our perimeter. With multiple family units, a known problem with enough food and such a rural location, we decided that 24x7 "guard duty" was not realistic.

We decided on game cameras that work with wireless internet. Of course, there is no wireless there and even if there was, you can't count on it working post-event. So we had to include our own wireless router in the design.

We have enough solar power available to run a laptop and the wireless receiver. The cameras will be installed so that we have almost full coverage of the outer perimeter. When they detect motion, the laptop will receive a picture, and sound an alarm.

Our egress ends up being an old barn, about ¾ of a mile away. We could pre-position some supplies there post-event during the grace period and I don't think anyone would find them.

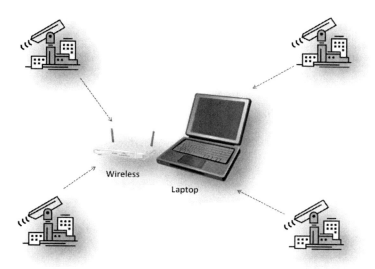

Wireless

Laptop

Figure 64 - EWS using Game Cameras for the Ranch

Our final analysis ended up with a location rating of 32.7, and our group rating was 23.5. Since we had pre-positioned supplies at our fighting positions, and have a good over watch, our Defense Rating came in at 29.46 – a good rating, but not as strong as I would like. We still have work to do and there will always be refinements, but I feel good about our plan.

Defensive Preparations	
Fighting Positions - Interior	3
Fighting Positions - Exterior	3
Over Watch	1
Defense Rating	**29.46**

Appendix A

If you are not familiar with spreadsheets, you can print out pages 12 and 13 and compute all of the values manually.

After the cells are filled in, here is how to compute the values:

Location Rating

A = ((Population Density * 50)*Proximity) + Physical Area

B = ((High Ground * .05) * Visibility) / Positions

C = (Open Access * 200) + (Limited Access * 100) + (No Access * 10)

Location Rating = ((A / B) / C) / 1000

Group Rating

A = (Basic Pistol + Basic Rifle + Mobile + Average + Basic Medical) * 100

B = (Advanced Firearms + Physically Fit + Aggressive + Engineer + Electronics) * 200

C = (Long Range Marksman + Combat Vet + Athletic + Medical + Hunter) * 300

D = (Trained Sniper + Has your back + Doctor) * 400

E = (Number of Dependents + Restricted Mobility + Timid)

Group Rating = ((A + B + C + D) / E) / 100

Defense Rating

A = (Fighting Positions Interior + Fighting Positions Exterior) + (Over Watch * 2)

Defense Rating = A + Group Rating – Location Rating

CPSIA information can be obtained at www.ICGtesting.com
Printed in the USA
LVOW130241301211

261707LV00004B/170/P

9 780615 497556